Also by Steve Almond

(Not that You Asked): Rants, Exploits,
and Obsessions

Which Brings Me to You
(with Julianna Baggott)

The Evil B.B. Chow and Other Stories

Candyfreak: A Journey Through the
Chocolate Underbelly of America

My Life in Heavy Metal

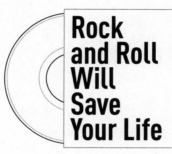

Rock
and Roll
Will
Save
Your Life

Steve Almond

Rock
and Roll
Will
Save
Your Life

A Book
by and
for the
Fanatics
Among Us

(with Bitchin'
Soundtrack)

RANDOM HOUSE 🏠 NEW YORK

Rock and Roll Will Save Your Life is nonfiction. I've changed a few names to protect the innocent and reconstructed certain conversations that took place many bongs ago. But all of it happened, especially the songs.

Published in the United States by Random House, an imprint of The Random House Publishing Group, a division of Random House, Inc., New York.

RANDOM HOUSE and colophon are registered trademarks of Random House, Inc.

The chapter "Winter in America with Gil Scott-Heron" was originally published in a different form in *The Believer*.

Permission acknowledgments can be found on page 221.

ISBN 978-1-4000-6620-9
eBook ISBN 978-0-6796-0365-8

Printed in the United States of America on acid-free paper

www.atrandom.com

9 8 7 6 5 4 3 2 1

First Edition

Book design by Liz Cosgrove

To Richard and Barbara Almond,
who continue to make beautiful music together.

We are ugly, but we have the music.

—Leonard Cohen

Contents

Rock
and Roll
Will
Save
Your Life

Bruce Springsteen Is a Rock Star, You Are Not

On a warm spring night three years ago, The Close called me up in a state of agitation. He had something I needed to see. This was a Tuesday, late, but I was at loose ends, meaning lonely and despicable. "Right," I said. "Let me find my pants."

The pants were necessary because The Close had moved across the Charles River into Boston proper, whereas I was still in Somerville, a city sometimes compared to Paris by people who have never visited either place. I suppose it's important to know that The Close and I were writers and that we spent most of our waking hours sitting at our keyboards making poor decisions, or cursing those poor decisions, or avoiding our keyboards altogether and feeling crushed by guilt, or (most often, actually) sitting at our keyboards not making any decisions at all because we were too busy cursing the obscurity to which we felt damned. Hey, it's a living. Also: while both of us had enjoyed years of misbehavior, the terrors of adulthood were now gently breathing down our necks in the form of our gentle fiancées, who were moving to town in a matter of weeks. Oh, and mine was pregnant.

The Close was smoking on the windowsill when I arrived. Nearby lay his binoculars, used to survey the windows of the building across the street for women in states of undress. He had one chair in his place, amid the Styrofoam take-out boxes and freshman compositions with titles such as "Why Raymond Carver Bores Me to Death." He gestured for me to sit and clicked on his VCR. "This is Bruce Springsteen playing the Hammersmith Odeon in 1975."

"Since when are you a Springsteen fan?" I said.

"Just fucking watch."

The Close was from Jersey and spoke the native tongue, a clipped, tough-guy patois that implied a life spent amid mobsters. This was (like so much else about The Close) patently fraudulent. He taught literature at a famous university and quoted the Terrible Sonnets of Gerard Manley Hopkins at least once an hour. Nonetheless, The Close was a creature of passion. He wasn't going to shut up until I watched.

The lights came up on the E Street Band, several of whom were wearing white fedoras. Springsteen appeared in black jeans and a tattered leather jacket. This was not the *Bruuuuuuuce* of recent popular imaginings: the airbrushed hunk with ass by Nautilus, or the elder statesman in dignified soul patch. No, this was Primordial Bruce, the scruffy kid with a goofy underbite and toothpick arms.

"Understand: *Born to Run* has just come out. Bruce is on the cover of *Time* and *Newsweek* the same week. They're calling him the future of rock and roll." The Close had his tongue practically inside my ear, jabbering these hot words of praise and envy. "The guy's got the world hanging off his dick and he's twenty-five years old. Can you imagine?"

"No," I said.

What struck me, in fact, was that Bruce looked frightened. He kept fidgeting with his cap and he refused to face the crowd. When he finally did speak, he sounded like a high school kid playing drunk.

"How's things going over here in England and stuff, huh? All right?" The crowd hooted and Bruce laughed so hard he began gasping for air. He wanted everyone to understand how outrageous he found the situation: all these posh Londoners turning up to see his little bar band. It was one of those awkwardly phony moments designed to conceal something awkwardly real. Bruce was stalling. He hadn't quite answered the question that haunts all budding superstars: *Do I have what it takes to be who they say I am?*

In the background, Roy Bittan played a piano run straight from the Motown playbook and Max Weinberg cracked at his drum set. Bruce staggered back to the microphone, only this time he spoke in a hushed growl. *Oh Christ,* I thought, *he's gonna try the black preacher thing.* "Yuh know, on the eighth day, He looked down on a bunch of drunks in this bar and uh—" Bruce wrestled the mic from its stand and again turned away from the crowd. "He looked down on a bunch of drunks in this bar on the eighth day, and, and with a wave of his hand he said . . .

Sparks fly on E Street when the boy prophets walk it handsome and hot

And suddenly Bruce was singing, urgent and raspy, and the crowd, released back into the music, erupted, because this was after all "The E Street Shuffle," Bruce's creation song, slowed to a half tempo, recast as an epic soul ballad, sent reeling back, that is, to its country of origin, the fuzzy AM radios in those big-finned cars he'd cruised as a lonely dropout punk, listening to Otis and Roy and Sam, dreaming he would someday be them: the man with the golden voice, the fearless band, who escaped his prospects not by forgetting where he came from but by commemorating its joys and hardships in song, and then, just in case anyone missed the point, Bruce steered his crew into a languorous version of "Having a Party."

The crowd was plowed. They'd never seen anything like Bruce, never seen a rock star swan dive from naked terror into poise, never heard a band reclaim American popular music with such raucous elegance. They played for two hours solid, culminating in a doo-wop rendition of "Quarter to Three" that ended (and started again) half a dozen times. Bruce twirled in the rosy light, soaked through and howling.

"Why the fuck should he stop?" The Close shouted into my earhole. "He's fucking *killing* those people. That's what I want, brother. Seriously. Enough of this shit." He gestured at the drafts scattered on his desk, the pitiful, noiseless words, then looked at me with his big sad Jersey eyes.

"Where the fuck did we go wrong?"

Yes, Where?

The Close expected me to say something wise, of course, because I'm his elder and because I frequently suffer from the notion that I have wise things to say. But it was past midnight by then and I was feeling just as wrecked as he was. We were, after all, in the twilight of our bachelorhood, our last hurrah as Dudes Who Might Be Anything, and so the perpetual adolescent dream of rock stardom had lashed up from the depths and seized The Close and he had called me because, well, misery loves another idiot with a jukebox where his soul should be.

Later, having driven home and heroically resisted getting stoned, I tapped out this e-mail:

> Now look here, Close: I recognize that what we do rarely lands us anywhere near the basic human plumbing of instinct. Whereas Bruce, he liberates the riot inside of us and shakes our butts for good measure. But you're a smart enough dope to recognize that all language is an aspiration to music. Our only refuge is that people need what we do, too, our own quieter songs.

Did The Close buy this horseshit? I would say no.

I certainly didn't. I couldn't shake the notion that we *had* gone wrong somewhere, that we belonged to some special category of the thwarted. We spent an inordinate number of hours mourning the fact that we had *not* wound up as rock stars or one-hit wonders or near-misses or bar bands or wedding bands or KISS cover bands.

We had wound up, instead, as wannabes, geeks, professional worshippers, the sort of guys and dolls who walk around with songs ringing in our ears at all hours, who acquire albums compulsively, who fall in love with one record per week minimum and cannot resist telling other people—people frankly not that interested—what they should be listening to and why and forcing homemade compilations into their hands and then calling them to see what they thought of these compilations, in particular the syncopated handclaps on track fourteen. For the purposes of dignity and common marketing, it would make sense to call us something catchy like, say, *Superfans*. But I'm going to nominate *Drooling Fanatics*, which better captures the embarrassingly regressive aspects of our tribe.

As a rule, DFs don't play an instrument. We don't even dance especially well, though we do jump up and down at live shows and scream an awful lot, usually the names of obscure songs the band recorded but never released in the States, or covers it performed as a lark on a cable access show nine years ago, a grainy video of which we tracked down online and now own. Our bright idea is that these outbursts will ingratiate us to the lead singer, or maybe the deadpan guitarist, and provoke an invitation to hang out backstage after the show.

Do we want to fuck the lead singer, or possibly the deadpan guitarist?

A fair question. If the DF in question is female, and the band is male, the answer is yes. If the DF is male, the answer is also yes, though to a lesser degree, determined by the taboos imposed on homosexuality in the mind and heart of the afflicted. The central desire, however, is not carnal. As noted, the DF would like, most of all, to *be* the lead singer or the deadpan guitarist, and would frankly settle for the fun-loving-but-not-terribly-thoughtful drummer.

What else?

DFs own at least three thousand albums at any given moment, with a core of our collection represented by any three of four configurations (digital, compact disc, vinyl, and cassette).

Despite a voracious appetite for new music, and a tragic misapprehension of our own cutting-edge tastes, we tend to attach ourselves to particular bands for long stretches, an affiliation that is both cloying and evangelical. We refer to band members by their first names. Friends, in turn, refer to band members as our "imaginary friends."

Chances are, we've loaned money to musicians.

Chances are, we were DJs in college and had a show with a name so stupid we are vaguely embarrassed to mention it now, though we are quite happy to mention that we were DJs in college.

Chances are we've spent weeks in puzzled anguish over why our favorite band isn't more popular, given how much the songs on the radio *suck*, though if our favorite band suddenly hit it big we'd feel more resentment than pride.

Chances are, the only periods of sustained euphoria in our lives have been accompanied by music.

No, Dude, I Really Mean It: Where'd We Go Wrong?

It's not a talent thing.

I'm almost sure it's not a talent thing. True, there are some folks who can't hit a note without doing violence to it, and others (such as my dear wife, Erin) who have trouble with the rhythmic intricacies of the ABC Song. And there are always those annoying few at the far end of the bell curve—your Mozarts and Paganinis—endowed with talents that make God seem awfully choosy.

But it is my entirely unscientific belief that most people are born with the basic tools to become musicians. Britney Spears, for instance, has an inoffensive voice and the ability to suspend large reptiles from her boobs. The making, or rendering, of popular songs is more a matter of determination than aptitude. The central allure of *American Idol* (a show I have not actually seen) resides in this notion. It *could* be us. A bit of practice, a good tooth scrub, a few Xanax . . .

Consider the hubbub over Susan Boyle, the forty-eight-year-old Scottish woman who appeared last year on the British version of *Idol*. Standing onstage for her audition, Boyle looked like a Monty Python in drag. Then she opened her mouth and this epic noise came ripping out of her. Within a week, she was the most celebrated person on earth, an Emily Dickinson for the Internet age. The fame pundits enlisted to inspect phenomena of this sort took pleasure in noting how Boyle repudiated our pathological devotion to youth and beauty, as if rooting for a homely woman were cause for self-congratulation. But they missed the essence of her appeal, which was (and is) the powerful fantasy that *a divine voice lurks within all of us*, ready to obliterate all our liabilities and doubts and transform us into the stars we know ourselves to be.

The reason we are not all rock stars is because most of us are unprepared to do the sort of sustained and lonely work that would allow us to learn an instrument, let alone the broader language of music, let alone how to suspend a large reptile from our cleavage. And then further unprepared to compose our own songs and to perform them in front of other people and to do so with enough gusto that we might compel someone—many someones, actually—to pay for a recording of our songs. It's a lot of labor, when you break it down. A lot of potential humiliation. So this book, though it will feature plenty of rock stars, and include many opinions related to rock stars, is centrally about what it's like to be a Drooling Fanatic.

Disappointing, I know.

But most of human history—the vast underside—is about people not getting to do what they truly want to do. Prehistoric man, for instance, wanted to eat and fuck and sleep in peace, and he almost never got to do that. The inhabitants of the early republics dreamed of liberty, but most spent their lives in the yoke. Those of us with the dumb luck to be born in what we call the "modern" "developed" world can pretty much eat and fuck to our hearts' content. We've got hours for dreaming, too, though a lot of that work has been outsourced to Hollywood. Consumption gets to be the star these days, because consumption pays the bills. I mean by this that American popular culture is almost entirely about consuming at this point and that any ideas or feelings expressed in the public domain arrive on behalf of products, generally with the gloss and subtlety of a fuck film. Welcome to the final stage of capitalism: porn.

But here's a little secret, between you, me, and the rest of the mall: buying shit isn't enough. What we wish for in our secret hearts is self-expression, the chance to reveal ourselves and to be loved for this revelation, devoured by love. And thus, most of us go about our duties of commerce and leisure in a state of perpetual longing, with nocturnal excursions into the province of despair.

This book is for those of us who have converted such unrequited desires into noble obsessions. It happens to be about music (as opposed to ice cream or Picasso or the Dallas Cowboys) because music came before anything else, before language and large-scale war and liquid soap, and because music is the one giant thing America has done right, amid all it has done wrong. Music, that ancient and incorruptible bitch.

This Book Will Contain

- Sometimes drunken interviews with America's finest songwriters
- The terrifying specter of Graceland stoned

- A brief examination of my wretched music criticism
- Recommendations you will often choose to ignore
- A reluctant exegesis of the song "Africa" by Toto
- Gratuitous lists

What Sort of Gratuitous Lists?

The sort rock critics are always making, only in reverse. For example:

Gratuitous List #1

Bands Shamelessly Overexposed by the "Alternative" Press

1. **Sonic Youth**
2. **Yo La Tengo**
3. **Radiohead**
4. **Velvet Underground**
5. **Nirvana**
6. **Beck**
7. **Bright Eyes**
8. **Pavement**
9. **Red Hot Chili Peppers**
10. **Sonic Youth**

These lists are *not serious*. They are inserted into the text merely as a way of pissing off the critics.

Anything We're Forgetting?

Oh, yeah. Thanks to the wonders of digital technology, this book allows you access to the world's first live-streamable CD, designed by me for the express purpose of eliciting your drool. All you have to do is go to www.stevenalmond.com and look for the button that says *Free CD!*

Having written these last two words I realize that you have now put this book down and gone to your computer—oh, you were already at your computer? okay—and begun streaming your *Free CD!* and listened to some of the tracks and maybe even forgotten about this book. Which is cool. I don't blame you. If I had a choice between a book and a CD, I'd do the same thing—and I write books for a living.

But assuming you've kept this book, I would ask that you hold off on listening to your *Free CD!* for a little while. The idea in my pointy little head is that you'll listen to the tracks as we arrive at them in the text.

Sure.

1

The DF Starter Kit (No Assembly Required!)

1. It helps considerably if your parents are musicians of some sort My mother, for instance, was an accomplished pianist who attended the High School of Music and Art before settling into the far more glamorous fields of parenting and psychiatry. In addition to her assigned roles as therapist, domestic slave, and mother to three savage monkeys (i.e. me, my twin brother, Mike, and our older brother, Dave) she played piano on a black upright Yamaha. Owing to the size of our home, the piano was located in what we savage monkeys thought of as the TV Room. This created a conflicting agenda, which in many ways crystallizes the generational dichotomy in our household: Mozart's *Piano Concerto No. 24 in C minor* versus *The Facts of Life*.

We barged in on her constantly, resentful of the attention she lavished on the instrument, and the serenity it seemed to grant her. Our father eventually affixed a latch to the door. Thus, the emblematic sound of our youth—a soft cascade of notes interrupted by ferocious pounding, then a muted sigh. Mom played beautifully.

Our father sang, starting in high school and later with the Harvard

Glee Club, a distinction we looked upon with the contempt to be expected of insecure male offspring. (Glee Club? Why not just announce you're in the *Gay* Club?) He performed *Lieder* mostly, accompanied by our mother. Our father with his chin tipped slightly up, mournful German couplets trembling from his chest. His throat swelling with imploration. Such vulnerability! We were mortified.

Our folks were too stuffed full of intellectual ambitions for a life in the arts. They were the descendants of European Jewry, cultured people who looked upon music as one of the elevating pleasures of our time on earth. They listened as much as they played, folk and rock music, but most of all classical.

We wanted nothing to do with classical music, excepting the Bugs Bunny episode "Rabbit of Seville," the viewing of which was as close as we came to a sense of musical communion with our father. He later dragged us to the actual opera, a decision he immediately regretted. Nonetheless, we could see how music soothed and transformed our parents and though we endeavored not to show them that we were impressed, we were and deeply.

2. *Display just enough musical talent to suffer lessons* I am flattering myself here, as is my wont. I did not have talent. What I had was a greater need for parental approval. I have no idea how piano was settled upon, though I'm sure my own Oedipal longings played a central role. My teacher was one Rosanna Sosoyev, a diminutive Russian émigré with a carefully arranged omelet of ginger hair.

Mrs. Sosoyev was what I'll call a "traditional" teacher. Before each lesson, she would inspect my hands, then send me to wash them. (On a few occasions, she marched me to the bathroom and washed them for me. This ritual—my hands in hers, the rose-scented soap, the warm water—was mildly erotic and deeply distressing.) She stressed scales.

Sosoyev: Now, we play the scale.

Me: [Playing, badly]

Sosoyev: Did you practice the scale this week?

Me: [Inaudible]

Sosoyev: You must practice the scale, Steven. You cannot play
the song without the scale. It is like the sturgeon. The sturgeon cannot swim with no scale.

Our lessons were like this: small, poorly attended battles of will.
The only spectator was her husband, a spectral figure who glided
from one room to another in a cloud of camphor. I like to imagine
that I caused Rosanna Sosoyev at least one small stroke, but I am
probably flattering myself again. My mother was the one who bore
the brunt of my halfhearted practicing. She had to listen to me
mangle Haydn sonatas night after night. I also smashed the keys with
my fists. A lot.

At a certain point, probably five or six years in, Sosoyev allowed me
to mangle a few of Scott Joplin's signature compositions: "Maple Leaf
Rag," "Peacherine Rag," "The Entertainer." I attacked these pieces
with grim and relentless determination. Mike referred to this as my
Maple Barf Rag phase.

It was no use. I sucked. I knew I sucked. If there was any confusion about my sucking (there wasn't) Sosoyev's annual recitals put
them to rest. Here, I was provided incontrovertible evidence that I
was making meager progress compared to her other pupils, who
regarded me with expressions of polite confusion. There seemed to
be some speculation that I was developmentally disabled.

What I lacked was the imagination that animates the learning
process. I kept waiting for that mystical moment when the underly-
ing grammar of music, the tonal relationships, would reveal themselves to me, or to my hands anyway, and I would suddenly just
know what to play without having to memorize which little piggy went

where and furthermore every key I hit would sound brilliant and glittery like Chico Marx. But this kept not happening because I refused to do all that lonely sustained work I mentioned earlier, because I lacked the capacity to forgive myself for mistakes (i.e. patience) and grew humiliated and angry and things turned smashy.

The sturgeon cannot swim with no scale.

3. Have an older sibling who thinks you're a dipshit   It's important that they think you're a dipshit because you're much more likely to worship them in this case, and to adopt their musical taste (which is better than yours) as a kind of gospel.

We need look no further than 1978, the year Styx was named America's Favorite Band by one of the many gold-plated award shows that slithered to prominence in the seventies. I remember this vividly because I raced to my older brother Dave's room with the news. He was the one who had turned me on to the mind-blowing brilliance of Styx and who I expected would share in my sense of personal vindication.

"Styx won best band!" I yelled.

"Styx sucks," he said quietly. "Get out."

I was dumbfounded. Styx *sucks*? But Styx so much *didn't suck*. Styx *ruled*. Styx were geniuses. They were like Mozart, like five Mozarts, each with diaphanous hair and shiny space-age jumpsuits, and they wrote pulsating anthems about renegade men and blue-collar men and epic ballads about love and loss and excessive cocaine use, none of which mattered because (inexplicably) Dave said they sucked.

A few days later I stole into his room and unearthed the culprit: an album called *Outlandos d'Amour* by the Police. What a disturbing artifact! Rock bands, after all, had mystical names like Led Zeppelin and Blue Öyster Cult. But the *Police*? I was a twelve-year-old whose hobbies were shoplifting and pyromania. Why would I listen to a band called the Police?

Nor did the songs make sense. They were jerky and tense, with minor-key melodies and jangled bursts of guitar. No solos. (Dude: *no solos?*) And the lyrics weren't about the reaper or invisible airwaves crackling with light. They were about loneliness and rejection, subjects on which I needed no additional briefing. I listened to *Outlandos d'Amour* straight through, trembling with disgust.

Why, then, did I keep sneaking into Dave's room and listening to the thing? If this were the sort of book written by a Professional Music Critic, I'd now be compelled to identify *Outlandos* as a watershed album, marking a shift from the bombastic escapism of prog rock to the edgy emotionalism of New Wave. I'd note the deft deployment of punk and reggae elements in a pop context and blah-blah-blah. But I'm a Drooling Fanatic. All I know is how I felt listening to the music: anxious and excited and weirdly relieved. There was this one song that was basically a long rant against an ex-girlfriend. *You'll be sorry when I'm dead,* the singer guy sang, *And all this guilt will be on your head.* When my dad heard these lines, he laughed. This was a funny song about being jilted, then committing suicide. Suicide could be funny. Equally shocking: rock music could be funny.

This is the big thing about having an older sibling; they're always pushing the nascent Fanatic to venture beyond the safe margins of his or her taste. Without meaning to (because honestly, they just want you out of their fucking room) they implant the vital notion that there is music out there you don't know about yet, and that you'd better get hip to, unless you want to remain an immature twerp who worships Styx.

But you can never catch up. That's the thing. Because your interest in a band is (to the older sibling) the essential indicator that band is over. You're the Casey Kasem of their existence. I chased Dave from the Police all the way out to the margins of punk, which explains how I came to conduct what probably ranks as the worst interview Jello Biafra ever endured—for our high school newspaper. Dave did manage to shake me off his trail, but he had to go over to the dark side to do it. He became a Deadhead.

4. Find a guardian angel So the older sib who thinks you're a dipshit is crucial, but any self-respecting DF needs a benevolent pusherman, too. Mine was Uncle Pete, my father's younger brother. Pete had tried out for the New York Yankees. He had been a TV reporter and made movies in Los Angeles. He had an apartment in New York City, a stunning new girlfriend every few years, the profile of a Greek god. He was practically a rock star himself.

On my tenth birthday, he presented me with *Songs in the Key of Life*. I listened to nothing else that fall. Every day after school, I sat with the album on my lap, trying to muster the courage to sing along with Stevie on "Have a Talk with God" and "I Wish" and especially "Village Ghetto Land." I didn't go to church or eat dog food. But I desperately wanted to be the kind of kid whose deprivation made me soulful rather than neurotic.

Pete kept up a steady supply: *Thunder Road, Shoot Out the Lights*. Then it was on to the advanced material—a compilation by Dion and the Belmonts, the dark ruminations of Leonard Cohen, the rambunctious poetry of Gil Scott-Heron. These albums were so far beyond my ken it took years to hear them properly. But I kept them with me. They were like savings bonds I knew would someday mature.

5. Be lonely, and spend your hours amid the lonely I didn't just like music. I needed music. There wasn't much else on my dance card. Pinball. TV. Masturbation, eventually. I spent a lot of time alone on the carpet in the living room, listening to *Abbey Road* or *Mind Games* or *Through the Past Darkly*. And studying these records, poring over the lyrics and album art. The back cover of *Goat's Head Soup*—with the actual goat's head in a cauldron of soup. I puzzled over that image for the entirety of 1975. (Could one actually make soup out of a goat's head? What would it taste like? What would happen to the horns and fur and teeth? And the eyes? Did one eat the eyes, or were they there just for flavor?)

Music was also a way of reaching out to friends, other boys mostly. It is in the nature of the pre- and adolescent male to isolate and brood, to interact as indirectly as possible, with aggressive ritual as mediation. These days, it's done with video games about carjacking. Back then, it was a devotion to particular albums. Scott Sutcher and I spent most of seventh grade locked in his room listening to *Dirty Deeds Done Dirt Cheap.* There was a protocol. He lay on the bed. I sat with my back against the box spring. We slammed Hostess products foraged from the pantry. There was almost no talking. A few words to fill the scratchy silence between songs. *You poot? You did. Dickwad. Pootwad.* Then it was back to the joyous malevolence of AC/DC, its perverted and fuzzy roar, the gravelly alliteration of the title track (all those croaked *D*s to which we chanted along so softly), the leering innuendo of "Big Balls," in which Bon Scott observes that some balls are held for "charity" and others for "fancy dress."

> *But when they're held for pleasure*
> *They're the balls that I like best*

Bon Scott delivered these lines with a smirking pomposity that struck us as unbearably sophisticated. The man was Byron. In the meatiest passages of particular songs, we closed our eyes and let the chords surge through us. It was a kind of trance. We were alone, but not alone. We were embarrassed—everything embarrassed us in seventh grade—but flushed with angry hopes.

When people bitch about the death of the vinyl LP as a medium (and lord knows they bitch) what they're mostly lamenting is the death of this kind of listening. Music as a concerted sonic experience, rather than the backing track to a flashing screen. What I'm suggesting here is that Drooling Fanaticism boils down to undivided attention, which is not only our most endangered human resource but the first and final act of love.

 Interlude:
Paradise Theater, American Classic

I mentioned Styx. Having done so, I cannot unmention them.

Let me say, then, that I loved Styx and that I still love Styx and not ironically either. There is no sin in the realm of taste. This will come as a shock to a critical establishment that prides itself on haughty judgment. But you can't tell someone his or her ears are wrong. You can't rescind the pleasure they derive from a particular piece of music. You can certainly deride that pleasure. If we were to meet and you were to break into the refrain of "Renegade," for instance, or "Come Sail Away," I would feel embarrassed. I might even, for the sake of camaraderie, go along with the gag. *Ha-ha-ha. Yeah, Styx: what was I thinking?* But that is quite different from what my body experiences when I listen to Styx. And in particular, when I listen to what I will now call—with no alcoholic intervention—the Styx masterpiece, *Paradise Theater.*

PT was released in the winter of 1981, my freshman year in high school. It documents the demise of Chicago's Paradise Theater, which is a *metaphor* for the demise of America's civic culture, which is *deep*, man. So it's a concept album, or half a concept album, because only Dennis DeYoung was committed to the concept and he was the pianist. The rest of the band almost certainly thought DeYoung was a fag.

That I memorized the album, word for word, will go without saying. That I used impromptu recitations to score titty privileges at Jewish summer camp also can be assumed. I was especially taken by the rousing power ballad "The Best of Times." I loved everything about it:

the Elton Johnish piano intro, DeYoung's histrionic vibrato, his shameless appropriation of Dickens, the marching cadence, the chorus with its richly harmonized coda ("These are the best . . . of *times*"), Tommy Shaw's Harrisonesque solo—a solo I cannot hear without picturing Shaw in the bright green jumpsuit he wore for the concert video: the Jolly Green Giant's tiny catamite lover. I dug every song on *PT*. The pulsing anthems ("Too Much Time on My Hands"), the weepers ("She Cares"), the obligatory coke addiction song ("Snowblind"), even DeYoung's corny piano outro. I bought the whole enchilada.

America *was* in decline, at least my version of America, and Styx got that. It chewed certain big ideas—dying cities, suburban atomization, a lost and shining past—into bite-size bromides, then set them to melodies that fell somewhere between the Monkees and Foreigner. It might be said that they lamented the homogenization of American culture while, in fact, homogenizing American culture. Or it might be said (if you were me) that they nailed the prevailing zeitgeist, the fraudulent nostalgia and grandiose self-regard of the Reagan era, the synthesized stunts and fluorescent, shoulder-padded duds. They made the listener feel good about everything, including the things one should feel bad about.

And let me take this a step further: if you want to know what people were thinking and feeling and dreaming in 1981, if you're curious about the emotional tenor of that particular slice of our history, *PT* is much more useful than any of the enduring LPs of that time, *Sandinista!* by the Clash, for instance, or U2's *October*. That's what makes it a classic. I still feel good when I listen to *Paradise Theater*. I feel I have, in some obscure manner, grappled with civilization and its discontents. I have registered my protest to the unkind march of time and danced the robot while doing so.

Critics never had much patience for Styx. They were the *apotheosis of late seventies prog-pop mediocrity*, and so forth. Nor has history been kind. Styx has become the mullet of bands. The band's real crime is not that they were too eager to please—though they were certainly that—but that they were too effective at pleasing. They got people to sing along. We all have a Styx in our closet, at least one. (Supertramp, anyone? Hootie & the Blowfish?) They're reminders of who we used to be, as surely as the feathered hair and Lycra bodysuits that haunt our old photo albums.

But my larger point is that there's no angle in hating on a particular song or band or genre. Our species is adaptable. That's our evolutionary trump card. If the human ear is given a chance, not cowed into snobbery, it can find rewards in almost any form of music. I think here of a line by Robert Christgau, who for many years represented the gold standard of rock critic snark. Assessing the work of Emerson, Lake & Palmer's *Brain Salad Surgery*, he wrote, "The sound is so crystalline you can hear the gism as it drips off the microphone." The line is funny, an appropriate epitaph for a trio that was Spinal Tappish in its pretense. But when I think about that album what I remember is sitting around with my pal Dale McCourt, listening to the endless onanistic glissandos and howled couplets of "Karn Evil 9" ("Welcome back my friends, to the show that never ends!"). We loved that song. And there's no arguing with joy.

2

Moving in Stereo

In 1984, I left California for Wesleyan University, in Middletown, Connecticut, ready to embrace the incredibly exciting musical options available to nascent Fanatics. Such as, for instance, Wang Chung and Wham! and Willie Nelson and Julio Iglesias and all the girls that Willie Nelson and Julio Iglesias had loved before, though presumably not at the same time. Madonna's undergarments were on MTV. Michael Jackson's head was on fire. Corey Hart was wearing his sunglasses at night. It was a confusing time.

I immediately fell in with the most confused guys on my freshman hall. Eric was a ska/punk aficionado (a skunker?) who tromped about in trench coat and porkpie hat, simmering with vaguely proletarian indignation. His favorite band was an obscure quartet called the Reducers, coastal Connecticut's answer to the Ramones. Davey was a math geek from central Jersey, with all the charisma that description implies. His hero was Scraping Foetus Off the Wheel (also known as You've Got Foetus on Your Breath). Industrial music, it was called.

We were all desperate for a show on the college station, WESU, but the orientation session was presided over by a cabal of pimpled upperclassmen who gave precedence to nubile frosh. Davey knew somebody who knew somebody, so he got a gig subbing on the overnight shift. I joined him in-studio, though he never let me talk into the mic, a foul-smelling lead device that hung pornishly over the soundboard. I was there to fetch him records, a pointless task given that all he ever played was Foetus, along with Frankie Goes to Hollywood's amphetamized cover of "Born to Run," which we both adored.

I can't remember a single class I took my first two years of college, let alone the ideas I was supposed to be absorbing. But I can remember with piercing aural precision my favorite songs: the jaunty fretwork that drove "Oblivious" by Aztec Camera, the sweet stuttered hook of They Might Be Giants' "Don't Let's Start," the ubiquitous fascist cabaret of Depeche Mode's "Master and Servant." Everyone was listening to the Smiths and the Cure. They were so romantically depressed, which seemed the thing to be, though I was more drawn to the horny angst of the Violent Femmes, whose debut was the lone cool album I already owned.

One day Davey played me a copy of Run-D.M.C.'s "Rock Box." It was the first rap song I'd ever heard and not at all representative of the genre, in that it was built around a guitar riff of Zeppelinesque enormity. Every time someone played the song in our dork kingdom I raced up and down the hall howling "Calvin Klein's no friend of mine, don't want nobody's name on my behind."

Sophomore year I moved with Davey to an off-campus apartment overlooking a Dunkin Donuts. The place smelled like fried dough until it began to smell like garbage, thanks to Davey, and I fled to Israel where I endeavored to give a shit about Judaism and stuffed falafel in my piehole and panted after a woman who turned me on to Suzanne Vega. Her debut album was just out and we listened to those dark delicate fairy tales constantly, talking late into the night about God and love and whether we were ever going to do it.

I climbed Masada that spring and floated in the Dead Sea and stowed away on a Greek ship. I walked past a Jerusalem pizza parlor half an hour before a bomb exploded inside. I humped poorly in various exotic locales. But the moment I remember as the most thrilling of that era was opening a package from my pal Evan and finding inside a bootleg of the Violent Femmes' third album, *The Blind Leading the Naked.*

The DJ Gene

It is my belief that human beings have something in their DNA that makes them crave control of their sonic environment such that long ago, in the valley of Neander, cavemen would invite each other over for a party and the host caveman would start beating out his favorite rhythm on, say, a stalactite, hoping to attract the attentions of the assembled caveladies, until one of his guests came up to him and suggested a different beat. The host, trying to appear casual, would say, "Yeah, that sounds cool. Maybe we can do that beat later," then resume drumming, at which point the other cavedude would press the matter—"Everyone's getting kind of, you know, *tired* of that beat"—at which point things turned ugly.

I have found nothing in the evolutionary literature to support this notion, though admittedly I have not yet inspected any of the evolutionary literature. Regardless, by junior year, my DJ Gene was pulsating violently. I had managed to insinuate myself into the WESU hierarchy by becoming a sports broadcaster, which led to my own predawn music show, and access to the thousands of LPs crammed onto the station's splintery shelves.

I was hopelessly intoxicated by the idea that I controlled the world's stereo system, along with a giant catalogue of music, much of it advance material that *no one had heard yet.* I showed up hours early for my show to browse the new releases. That's how I found *All Fools Day*, an album of swaggering Celtic soul by an Australian quartet

called the Saints. That's also how I found *Folksinger,* by Phranc, a lesbian folksinger with a flattop who crooned about celebrity coroners
and female mud wrestling. After my show, I took these records into
the auxiliary studio and listened to them over and over until one of
the techies, in a moment of uncharacteristic pity, showed me how to
copy records onto cassette. It was like hunting for treasure, particularly if I went trolling in the massive, unkempt archives where, one
lucky morning, I stumbled across an old Fleshtones record that
included the track "Hexbreaker," a rousing anthem that sounded like
the MC5 crashing headlong into Otis Rush.[1] I played it at least once a
show.

I also began hitting up friends for musical tips. I was a resident
adviser that year (official hall motto: *Nothing That Could Get Me Sued*)
and one of my frosh—a Beverly Hills hipster—slipped me the debut
album by a Scottish quartet called Del Amitri, recorded when the lead
singer was about twelve. It was (and is) a perfect pop record: a brisk
journey into romantic ruin. It wasn't enough that I loved Del
Amitri—or the Femmes or the Saints or Phranc—I needed everyone
to love them.

Why? Why wasn't it enough for me to enjoy these fine musicians?
Why did it immediately become *my* job to spread the good news? It's
a question that plumbs the heart of the Drooling Fanatic. There's the
genetic explanation, of course. And the younger-brother-chip-on-my-
shoulder thing. But my compulsion had a tangled erotic aspect, too. I
wanted to feel a certain kind of possession. Like any crush, it was
partly about the narcissism of my own desire. And it was more than

---

1. This description is a prime example of what I call an Obnoxious Rock Critic
Moment (ORCM, pronounced *or*-kum). It is intended to suggest a false degree of
sophistication via fancy words and/or allusions the lay reader probably doesn't recognize, and which are not sonically precise but look good on paper. In the present case,
though citing the MC5 makes sense, I have only a vague idea of who Otis Rush is—
blues player, old, black?—because I was under the impression that he recorded the
song "You Make Me Wanna Shout," when, in fact, it was the Isley Brothers.

that. I wanted other people to feel what I felt, inside, when those songs came on. Deep down I saw them as a solution to the crisis of my loneliness.

Reluctant Exegesis:
"(I Bless the Rains Down in) Africa"

I said before that there is no objectively "bad" music. I must now amend that statement. In so doing, let me cite Duke Ellington, who once famously declared that "there are only two kinds of music: good music and bad music. And by bad music I mean specifically the song '(I Bless the Rains Down in) Africa' by Toto." Ellington died two years before Toto formed as a band, which speaks to his prescience.

What makes "(I Bless the Rains Down in) Africa" so bad? Mostly, it's the lyrics. Also, the instrumentation, the vocals, and that virulent jazz-lite melody, which, despite the manifest wretchedness of everything I've just mentioned, means that you are no doubt conjuring the song even as you read this—those hypnotic banks of synthesizer and phony "tribal"-sounding drums—and without at all meaning to, sort of . . . grooving to "(I Bless the Rains Down in) Africa," sort of digging it, sort of bathing in the buttery memory of sixth grade or tenth grade and hand jobs and lip gloss and really actually kind of remembering, or rediscovering, how much you *love* "(I Bless the Rains Down in) Africa" even as you're hating yourself for this love. It's complicated.

So are the lyrics:

I hear the drums echoing tonight
But she hears only whispers of some quiet conversation
She's coming in 12:30 flight
The moonlit wings reflect the stars that guide me towards salvation

Our hero is waiting for a female whose plane arrives just after midnight. Got it. This seems to place him in or around an airport, the sort of airport within earshot of drums. He can see the wings of the plane, which are lit by the moon and also, curiously, able to reflect stars.

> I stopped an old man along the way
> Hoping to find some long forgotten words or ancient melodies
> He turned to me as if to say, "Hurry boy, it's waiting there for you"

Suddenly our hero is no longer waiting around some poorly sound-proofed airport. No, he's on a journey, presumably outside. He encounters an unidentified old man. Contrary to the dangling modifier, it is the speaker, not the old man, who is hoping to find some long-forgotten words or ancient melodies. The old man will supply these, because the old man is African and all Africans, by definition, possess ancient melodies. The old African then turns to our hero. It is a complex physical gesture, one that manages to convey a vital and perhaps ancient truth: *our hero must hurry!* Why? Because "it's waiting there" for him. What is "it"? Where is "there"? Only the old African knows for sure.

> It's gonna take a lot to drag me away from you
> There's nothing that a hundred men or more could ever do
> I bless the rains down in Africa
> Gonna take some time to do the things we never had

We now have reached the swelling chorus, in which our hero, still awaiting his plane-bound paramour and, at the same time, questing "there" in search of "it," confesses his devotion to an unknown love object that we can only assume is the female on the plane. This devotion is stronger than a fairly sizable militia. It is a devotion so overwhelming, in fact, that our hero—well, you already guessed this, didn't you?—*blesses the rains down in Africa*. This tells us two things. First, he is north of Africa. Second, he is in a position to bless rain.

The sudden introduction of Africa as a thematic element might seem dissonant, but is easily explained by the "Africa" creation story, as related by Toto keyboardist David Paich: "Over many years, I had been taken by the UNICEF ads with the pictures of Africa and the starving children. I had always wanted to do something to connect with that and bring more attention to the continent. I wanted to go there, too, so I sort of invented a song that put me in Africa. I was hearing the melody in my head and I sat down and played the music in about ten minutes. And then the chorus came out. I sang the chorus out as you hear it. It was like God channeling it. I thought, 'I'm talented, but I'm not that talented. Something just happened here!'" Paich then worked on the lyrics for another six months.

> *The wild dogs cry out in the night*
> *As they grow restless longing for some solitary company*
> *I know that I must do what's right*
> *Sure as Kilimanjaro rises like Olympus above the Serengeti*
> *I seek to cure what's deep inside, frightened of this thing that I've*
> *   become*

Our hero is now clearly located in Africa, a place David Paich would very much like to go. We know this because there are wild dogs that cry out at night. It's unclear why these dogs would seek "solitary company" or what "solitary company" might be, but never mind—Paich only had six months to work on the words. The dogs remind our hero that he is on a quest. In fact, he has a moral obligation whose looming presence he compares to a famous mountain rising like another famous mountain over a famous desert, although, intriguingly, the mountain in question does not actually rise above the desert in question because it is several hundred miles away. Regardless, our hero is struck by the realization that he is sick. He's become a thing of which he is frightened. It remains unclear whether finding "it" "there" will remedy this deep-seated thingdom.

What is clear at this point in the song is that David Paich recognizes the unique versatility of the word "thing," which here alludes to a person of indeterminate turpitude while elsewhere serving as a noun simultaneously representing activities and possessions.

Hurry boy it's waiting there for you
It's gonna take a lot to drag me away from you
That's nothing that a hundred men or more could ever do
I bless the rains down in Africa, I bless the rains down in Africa
I bless the rains down in Africa, I bless the rains down in Africa
I bless the rains down in Africa

Our hero now reiterates his spiritual bond to Africa.

Dear Drought-Plagued Continent, he is saying. *You really remind me of this chick I want to sleep with. Something about you—maybe it's the wild dogs or the ancient melodies or the starving children I watch on TV— makes me realize I've been working too hard. I need to give myself more time to do and consume things with my lady, who I wish would get here already. In return, I bless your rains.*

There are, of course, many muddled romantic fantasies with artificial backdrops in the pantheon of pop music. The remarkable thing about this one is that it expresses so many quintessentially American attitudes at once:

1. The consumption of televised suffering grants me moral depth
2. Benevolence begins and ends in my imagination

3. Africa sure be exotic

4. All this consuming and appropriating is tiring—break time!

Rather than exposing us to the hard-won truth of individual experience, the song immerses us in the Karo syrup of an entire culture's mass delusion. It is the lovechild of Muzak and Imperialism.[2]

2. Did any of this dawn on me during the winter of 1983, as I wooed the lovely and freckled Ali Vickland in a variety of suburban parking lots? *Hell* no. I knew only that "Africa" was the ideal song for advancing my sexual agenda, in that it was catchy in a quiet-storm sort of way and implied that I was worldly and perhaps socially conscious and therefore—by some mysterious adolescent calculus best left unparsed—could be trusted not to talk publicly about the size and shape of her boobs.

How I Became a Music Critic

I very much wish I could skip over the part of the story where I take voice lessons and join a gospel choir. You really don't want to hear about this, especially if you're me. The short version:

Having failed at piano—and putting aside a disastrous stab at saxophone—I decided late in college that I would follow in my father's footsteps by singing. The only lesson I can remember in any detail is the week I attempted to sing "Country Death Song" by the Violent Femmes. The tune is about an insane hillbilly who throws his daughter down a well, and is sung in the manner one would associate with insane hillbillies, which is to say not a manner one would associate with formal voice training. I believe this is what appealed to me about the song. My voice teacher's expression was the sort you see on certain trauma patients.

Did I give up? No. That's my problem. I don't give up enough. Instead, I joined Wesleyan's gospel choir, the Ebony Singers. I was allowed to do so thanks to a shortage of black men willing to sing the bass parts. Our section consisted of me and three other white guys. Picture a barbershop quartet. Now picture them surrounded by black women howling about the blood of the lamb. Now picture the white guys trying to clap along and stomp their feet. Now stop.

My career as an Ebony Singer was meteoric, in the sense that something large and flaming (my ego) crashed into something larger and unhappy (an audience). This was the result of the choirmaster's baffling decision to allow me to perform a solo in concert. I settled on a pitch two octaves above my natural range. I also did a little James Brown clinch with the mic. If the Aryan Nation were in the market for a Moment of Supreme Whiteness, I believe I provided one. And nobody got hurt, if you don't count the crowd.

Bob Dylan Is Also, Unbeknownst to Me, a Rock Star

Having by now established my bona fides as a nonmusician, it's time to outline my career as a bitter hack, which begins with a summer internship in the sports department of the *Peninsula Times Tribune*, Palo Alto's hometown daily. One afternoon, the City Editor stood up in the middle of the newsroom and announced that the music critic was sick and he needed someone to review the Bob Dylan concert that night.

There was nobody around, aside from the sports goons and the mushrooms on the copy desk—populations deeply, almost tenderly, committed to the avoidance of discretionary labor. I alone volunteered. As a reminder: I was the intern in the sports department. I had written exactly one story for the paper. It was about luge. The City Editor closed his eyes and pressed the heel of his palms into the sockets. "You know anything about Dylan?" he said finally.

Did I know anything about Dylan? What did I *not* know about Dylan?

The City Editor exhaled through his nose. "Fine."

Alas, one of the few things I didn't know about Dylan was who, exactly, he was. So it was off to the library, where people went before

God invented the Internet and where I discovered that Dylan had recorded 150 albums. I had four hours to memorize them.

The show was at the Shoreline Amphitheater, a venue built atop a landfill in Mountain View. Dylan had just released *Knocked Out Loaded* and would soon join the Traveling Wilburys. It was not a good time for him, though I didn't know that. I found a seat on the grass and started taking notes (i.e. I scribbled adjectives that seemed to bear some relation to the songs he was performing). Only I didn't know the names of the songs he was performing. I had to lean over and ask my neighbors, though I waited until after Dylan had finished a song because my neighbors were all Drooling Dylan Fanatics, though often Dylan tore through three or four songs in a row which meant I had to get the rundown from my neighbors before the next burst of songs, and frantically scribble arrows (in the dark) to indicate which adjectives applied to which song titles, along with observations of *significant physical detail*, such as, "Dylan stares at crowd" and "Dylan turns away from crowd" and "Dylan appears to need a blood transfusion."

(Presto Chango) I Am Now a Rock Critic

I will remind the gentle reader that I was nineteen at the time of this review. I did not know who Bob Dylan was. I had no technical training as a musician—if you don't count the Sosoyev years, which you shouldn't. Had I been quizzed on the meaning of the word *glissando* I would have answered (with some confidence, I'm afraid) "a type of fancy ice cream." Not to be confused with *vibrato*, which was a gynecological instrument. And yet, as far as the readers of the *Peninsula Times Tribune* were concerned, I was a professional critic.

If this sounds absurd, consider the proposition that greeted me when I arrived at the *El Paso Times* two years later, fresh from college. Would I like to be the paper's music critic? Of course I would. It was like being handed a license without having to take any exams, a license that granted me front-row tickets to all the big concerts, and phone interviews during which I could indulge in the fantasy that, for example, Edie Brickell and I really *were* pals, based on our intense twenty-minute tête-à-tête, and that she really meant it when she urged me to stop by her trailer "to say hey," and that if things went well in her trailer—which they very well might, thanks to my dazzling prose and chestal pelt—we would wind up engaged in a sweaty duet on top of an amp, an indiscretion she'd obviously try to write off as a fling except that she'd be unable to forget that tall, virile music critic from the West Texas town of El Paso, meaning more breathy phone calls, more visits, an eventual leak to the press, and a clandestine elopement captured by *People* magazine. As it is, Brickell wound up married to Paul Simon, a man much shorter than myself.

Also: I was suddenly up to my eyeballs in free music. I could call any record company on earth and direct them to send me an album. The only downside—and it was a rather large downside—involved El Paso's unique geography, which can be best captured by the sign that greeted me as I drove into town for the first time:

EL PASO   11
SAN ANTONIO 592

Which is to say, El Paso is located in a rather remote part of the world from the American perspective, one very few concert promoters book, unless they work with country or heavy metal stars. Because El Paso is on the border with Mexico, a good number of Latin music acts also came to town, in particular Menudo, whom I reviewed three times. (If you have ever tried to make time with a grown woman by offering her a front-row seat to a Menudo concert, I propose we start a support group.)

Every year or so I got to review a band I liked, such as R.E.M. or Concrete Blonde or Steve Earle. But for the most part I was writing about Winger and Alabama and Reba McEntire and Vixen and Poison and George Strait, whom I reviewed four times, making me the only

Jew (that I know of) to have his work excerpted in *The George Strait Newsletter.*

The coolest band I ever got to review was Los Tigres Del Norte. Los Tigres was considered a *norteña* band, *norteña* being that jaunty, synthesized stuff that blares from the storefront speakers of border towns. But Los Tigres played everything: waltzes, boleros, *cumbias*, and their songs were really short stories about immigration and drug trafficking, about the desperation of living in a poor country hard up against a rich one. I can remember sitting high in the bleachers of the El Paso County Coliseum, amid the *viejos* swigging from dented flasks, as down below five thousand couples danced, the women beaming in pink and green dresses, twirling like bright ribbons around their shy mustached men.

I should mention, mostly for the sake of my own embarrassment, that I was called upon to review many other genres about which I knew next to nothing, such as jazz and classical, the latter including a young harpist whom I inevitably compared to Harpo Marx. My central concern as a critic wasn't the music, but the mechanics of hitting my deadline. Specifically, would the Radio Shack TRS-80 upon which I worked crash before I could attach it to the "modem." This was a giant rubber phone cuff that somehow whisked the words from my portable computer to the newsroom. It all seemed quite magical back in 1989.

Did it ever occur to me to learn more about music? Not really. Technical expertise could be established by using a word such as "polyrhythms" from time to time, but it wasn't required. I worked for a Gannett paper. The whole point was to write at a fifth-grade level.

The Rock Crit Paradox

Am I making excuses for being such a lazy and frankly suckass reviewer in El Paso? Yes. But I was also, in my own frankly suckass way, up against an ontological dilemma: the description of one sort of language (physical, auditory, intuitive) by another (abstract, intellectual, symbolic).

Talented critics can, of course, describe music with sonic precision. Take, for example, this passage from Sasha Frere-Jones's review of the Canadian singer Feist in *The New Yorker*, a magazine I keep stored in my bathroom for research purposes:

> The song is built around Feist's vigorous acoustic-guitar strum: she plays like a street busker, strong on the downstroke and evenly loud. A three-note motif on a glockenspiel and an organ runs through the song, softening the forward motion of the guitar. In a short chorus, the guitar stops and Feist sings harmony with herself: "Ooh, I'll be the one who'll break my heart, I'll be the one to hold the gun." Then Gonzales plays a rising and falling two-note ostinato on the piano, subtly coloring the song. The accretion of felicitous musical details is typical of the album's smart, unfussy arrangements.

Frere-Jones is certainly not messing around. He covers instrumentation, performance style, and lyrical content. True, he risks losing those of us who are musical dolts, but it certainly didn't kill me to look up the word *ostinato*, which means "a musical phrase persistently repeated at the same pitch" and which I plan to incorporate into every discussion I have for the next ten years. The real problem here is emotional. The prose, for all its technical fidelity, conveys almost nothing about what the music *feels* like.

Consider the famous chord progression that Angus Young plays at the beginning of "Back in Black." A good writer could tell us about those grinding, seismic chords, the distinct rhythm of their deployment, even that sly, arpeggiated little five-note lick that acts as a segue from one volley to the next. But those are just pale approximations of what it *feels* like to hear that intro, the squirt of sinister glee that ˙

makes most people—even decent religious folk—reach for their air guitar.

Now consider the rest of the song: the rhythmic structures (bassline, drums), Brian Johnson's howling vocal, harmonic and tonal relationships, etc. But okay, let's say you've taken your Rock Crit Steroids and you're able to describe all these elements. How, then, do you convey the *simultaneity* of all that noise, the blissful riot of sound we experience as a singular thing (the song)? But okay, okay, let's say you've taken your Rock Crit Steroids for years, you're the Barry Bonds of Rock Crit, and so you manage to get this, too. You'd still be left with the Basic and Insoluble Crisis of Melody: words cannot be made into notes. And even if you somehow magically solved that crisis (which you couldn't) you'd still be missing what it feels like for a particular fan to hear a particular song (let alone songs, let alone in concert) because this involves a collaboration between the music and the fan's own needs: his or her own lust for joy, sorrow, power, rage, sex, and— oh what the hell—hope.

I know this from my time in the trenches, those hundreds of nights I spent with the kids who camped out overnight for tickets, or got scalped, the shy, tattered metalheads from Juárez who forked over a month's salary for the chance to see Queensrÿche live. (Your global economy at work!) If you asked those kids to review the concert you'd get emphatic grunts. *Rad! Killer!* Which would be overstating the case, because their experience of the event wasn't about words at all, but the annihilation of words, a fleeting return to primal self-expression when it was enough to bay like a wolf at the accretion of felicitous musical details.

The closest I came to grappling with the Rock Crit Paradox was at an MC Hammer concert. I stood beneath the stage watching Hammer twitch in his weird Sinbad jodhpurs while a battalion of dancers in identical Sinbad jodhpurs replicated his every twitch. Hammer barked lyrics about jewelry and torture. The melodies, sampled from bubblegum hits, affixed themselves to the artillery of drum machines. Lights popped and scrolled. Sparks vomited from some invisible portal. It was like watching an ad for a delicious soda that makes people want to commit murder. This was all quite clear to me. I'd even come up with a name for this soda.[3] But then I looked at the people around me, there in the fifth row of the Pan Am Center in Las Cruces, New Mexico. They were all dancing wildly. Hooting at the sweaty-boobed flygirls and barking along with Hammer and (without even realizing it) mimicking little Hammerish flourishes: the frenetic Egyptian jazz hands and his mincing bucklestep. These people were plugged into a powerful communal experience. They didn't look upon MC Hammer as a musical huckster, but an entertainer of the first rank and maybe even, in a sense, a prophet of self-assertion, proof that any man endowed with sufficient determination—no matter how meagerly endowed with talent—might gain trespass into the kingdom of fame. Yes, I was stoned.

Still, it was clear my fellow congregants were having a radically different experience from the assigned critic. So I wrote two reviews that night, which ran side by side the next morning: one from my perspective (i.e. one that cold-cocked Hammer) and one from the perspective of the fans (i.e. one that fellated Hammer). This struck me as perhaps the cleverest thing anyone on earth had ever done. Pleasantly, copies of the reviews don't exist to contradict me.

A Brief, Not Entirely Hopeful Note for Aspiring Music Writers

It is certainly worth asking, amid this whinging, whether it is possible to write about music in a manner that doesn't invite pity or derision. The answer is yes. Here's a lovely paragraph I came across recently:

3. Blüdthirsty.

All night the saxophones wailed the hopeless comment of the Beale Street Blues while a hundred pairs of golden and silver slippers shuffled the shining dust. At the gray tea hour there were always rooms that throbbed incessantly with this low, sweet fever, while fresh faces drifted here and there like rose petals blown by the sad horns around the floor.

How does one learn to write about music with such grace and precision? Easy! All you have to do is be F. Scott Fitzgerald writing *The Great Gatsby*.

Interlude:
Why Covering the Grammys Is Not as Glamorous as You May Have Been Led to Believe

It was this same year, 1989, that my editor sent me to cover the Grammys. I can't remember the exact lie I told to induce this very poor editorial decision, but I'd be willing to bet that it involved implying that one or more of the nominees were from El Paso. George Michael, for instance. Eric Clapton, Frank Zappa, Sting, Iggy Pop. All native El Pasoans. Oh, and Taylor Dayne. She was actually born in Juárez.

By the time my editor got wise to my—what is it that we're supposed to call lies these days? . . . Ah yes, my *mis-statements*—I was winging my way to L.A. My duties entitled me to press credentials, a commemorative Grammy Awards Tote Bag, and (as a bonus gift in this final year of the eighties) a vial of cocaine. Cell phones didn't exist yet, so I had to use a pay phone to call every single person I knew and tell them I wouldn't be available for the next few days because I was *covering the Grammys*.

Here's what I figured would happen: I'd arrive at the Shrine Auditorium and there'd be this giant diamond-studded vacuum device which would suck me into the inner sanctum of The Music Industry, a softly lit pillow lounge sort of place where Prince and Springsteen would be jamming with the remaining Beatles and someone would hand me a drink and I'd get spun into the arms of Linda Ronstadt, who would be dressed in a mariachi garter-belt type ensemble and who would muss my hair in aroused proto-cougar fashion and reach into my back pocket and toss my reporter's notebook away and laugh girlishly, then whisper into my ear that her "needs" would have to be met before she could go out and do her song, and by the way could Toni Tennille tag along?

In the event, I spent three hours standing in line outside the Shrine Auditorium, the wrong line it turned out, a line intended for those media with "floor credentials," which explained why the others in line were so tan and nicely dressed and attractive, why they had monstrous heads and blinding teeth and hair that didn't move: they were TV reporters. The situation was clarified by a kindly security official named DeWayne, who directed me to a second, much uglier line in the back of the building, located downwind from the septic outflow. Ah yes, the Shrine Auditorium's anus.

The Shrine's lower intestine awaited, a cavernous hall with folding tables and chairs and not quite enough outlets or phone jacks for the pack of unhappy print journalists who were—if our expression of collective bafflement was any indication—uncertain as to how we were supposed to view the Grammys. This mystery was solved when a green-jacketed official wheeled out a video screen. We would be watching the Grammys on TV.

It was a bit more dodgy than that, though, because we could hear a muffled version of the live performances from the main hall, then, after a seven-second tape delay, the broadcast version. Pretty much any song will drive you insane if staggered in this way, but none quite so quickly or convincingly as Metallica's "One."[4]

---

4. The song is about a blind and deaf quadriplegic boy. Imagine the Who's "Tommy" without any major notes and told from the point of view of the pinball.

As members of the press, we were allowed to interview the winners in an officially licensed Grammys Holding Pen. But getting quotes meant we had to stop watching the broadcast, which was not an option, given that we had nothing upon which to predicate our panicky dispatches *but* the broadcast.

As a reminder, this was 1989. The most popular album in America was George Michael's *Faith*. The second most popular album was the *Dirty Dancing* soundtrack. Rap music had just been recognized as a category and Kool Moe Dee celebrated by allowing someone not very kind to dress him in an electric blue ensemble, with bowtie. The sight of him was rivaled in sadness only by Sinéad O'Connor, who was forced to lip synch while gyrating anorexically in a halter top.

Was there drama? Yes. As it emerged, the two artists who dominated the night were Tracy Chapman and Bobby McFerrin (both El Paso natives!). Chapman had released a stark and lovely debut album that included "Fast Car," a single I had played *more than a year earlier* on my college radio show. McFerrin's claim to fame was the a cappella calypso "Don't Worry, Be Happy." Everyone had loved "Don't Worry, Be Happy" for about a week, before realizing it made them want to puke.

Chapman won Best New Artist, Best Female Vocalist, and Best Folk Artist. She was up for all three major awards—Album, Record, and Song of the Year—and it seemed obvious to everyone (if by everyone, I can be taken to mean me) that she was going to sweep these. So I wrote my story predicated on this assumption, then began calling my friends from press row.

What happened next? I noticed the guy beside me, a loquacious correspondent for what he called "the majorest news magazine in entire Panama," conducting a heated phone discussion in Spanish with his editor, during which he made many references to *Bobi McFar-rrring*, each preceded by what I assumed to be a colorful Panamanian curse word. I glanced at the TV monitor. There was Bobi, collecting the Grammy for Record of the Year. Then he won Song of the Year.

At this point, my phone began ringing. The chief copy editor wanted to know why (in the fuck) I had submitted a story identifying Tracy Chapman as the winner of these awards. I urged her to remain calm. Tracy Chapman was a shoo-in for Album of the Year. "Trust me," I said. "I'm the music critic."

Album of the Year went to George Michael's *Faith*.

There is no need to revisit the ensuing editorial discussions. Instead, I'll skip to the moment when—having been quietly excreted from Shrine Auditorium and driven lost for two hours around Los Angeles—I arrived at the apartment of my pal Mark, upon whose futon couch I was glamorously crashing. "What happened to *you*?" he asked.

Right.

The predictable thing at this point would be for me to assail the Grammys, to say something like, oh, for instance, "The Grammys are nothing more than some gigantic promotional machine for the music industry. They cater to a low intellect and they feed the masses." But it turns out that somebody already said this, namely Maynard James Keenan, the lead singer of the rock band Tool. It is probably worth noting that Tool has won three Grammys. Nonetheless, Mr. Keenan, you are right! The Grammys do cater to a low intellect and feed the masses. *That's why they exist.* Mr. Keenan's crucial error—I'm not counting his decision to name his band Tool—resides in his expectation that televised award shows reflect artistic merit. They exist to generate revenue. As such, they are potent expressions of the American spirit, nearly as potent as "Don't Worry, Be Happy."

List #2

Ten Things You Can Say to Piss Off a Music Critic

1. Sonic Youth—are they the ones that do "Pass the Dutchie"?

2. People who don't like Steve Miller should fucking move to Canada.

3. Jack Johnson is our generation's Woody Guthrie.

4. Don't you sometimes wish "Free Fallin'" were the national anthem?

5. Do me a favor and hold my beer. Thanks, dude. I'll be right back.

6. Yeah, but have you ever seen Michael Bublé play *live*?

7. Don't you wish these jazz dweebs would learn to play a *real* song?

8. *Exile on Main Street* is okay, but it's no *Steel Wheels*.

9. Did you ever want to be, like, a musician yourself?

10. *Paradise Theater* is an American classic.

Configurations (or How The Industry F'd Us)

Back in fourth grade, Alissa Fox brought to class a miraculous device her father supposedly helped invent. It had a numerical keyboard and performed all four basic math functions, with the results visible (sort of) on a tiny gray screen. Of especial interest was the fact that you could turn the machine over and type a secret series of numbers, so as to produce words such as "hello" and "boobs" and "bigboobs." This machine—called a *cal-cu-lator*—so totally blew our minds that it was assumed that Alissa Fox's dad was in the CIA and could shoot lasers from his teeth.

Back when I was teaching undergrads how to write short stories that would horrify their parents, I often told this story, in an effort to compel my classes to think about how quickly technology has transformed our species, has shifted our attention from individual imaginative tasks to collective screen addiction and thereby replaced the peculiar sensitivities of our internal lives with a series of frantic buy messages. One of my students would eventually respond to this by smiling timidly and saying, *Man, you're really old.*

Yes I am. I'm so old, in fact, that I've experienced all five of the major configurations by which recorded music is received. (I exclude the player piano, which predates me by several months.)

The Phonographic Era (1966–1979)

Things I loved about vinyl records:

1. They were large, pitched to the scale of their emotional importance. You could sit them in your lap. You could study their intricacies without squinting, which was essential because it was impossible to understand the songs without having decoded the messages embedded in the album art, e.g. the significance of the four cards held by the mustached magician on Blue Öyster Cult's *Agents of Fortune*, which Dale McCourt insisted represented the Four Horsemen of the Apocalypse, while his nemesis Gary Lahr said, no, they were tarot cards representing death and the grim reaper (somehow distinguishable) and, if memory serves, the Holy Grail.

2. Albums were fragile and therefore precious. You had to hold them by the edges, and flip them with great caution and slip them into their special paper sleeve before filing them away. You couldn't take them places. You couldn't leave them outside. They warped.

3. They exuded a faint and intoxicating cardboardy odor.

4. They invoked *a process*. You didn't just press a button. You had to interact with the technology in minimal but crucial ways, not so much by dropping the album onto the turntable, which anyone could do, but by lowering the needle onto the record, which you could only do if you were old enough. What excruciating pleasure! To set the tip of one's index finger under the arched band extending from the end of the stylus, then transport that feathery aluminum arm (with its glamorous and barely visible tip) toward the spinning record! There was a right way to do this and a thousand wrong ways and the results were amplified. If you got the yips, the needle went screeching across the record. If you missed the thin band of ungrooved vinyl, you landed in the middle of a song. If you dropped the arm from too high

you produced a crisp *pop*, known in the parlance of my crowd as popping a goochie. (*You yipped it, gooch.*)

And the needle—the needle was not to be touched! The needle was MADE OF DIAMOND. Diamond was the hardest substance on earth. And yet the needle was the most fragile object on earth. How could this be? *It just was.* Touch the needle and the house will collapse around you. Your cat will burst into flames. Your parents will start having sex right in front of you on the living room rug for an hour. The most you could do was blow on the needle, so as to remove the dust gathered thereon, and even this was risky. (*You fucking loogied on the needle, gooch.*)

But if you got the needle onto the record? Suddenly, the air around you was painted with sound. You had engineered a miracle, an intricate mechanism of conversion visible to the naked eye. You could track the minute dips and risings of the needle over the grooves, something I did religiously, until I had discerned the precise spot where the wispy jet engine that opens "Back in the U.S.S.R." was interrupted by the thrilling squawk of George Harrison's guitar. If you lost yourself in a record, lay back and closed your eyes, you would eventually reach the distant surf at the end of each side.

The effect was never the same with 45s, which I listened to as a very young boy. I hated 45s, not just because of those loathsome self-vaporizing yellow inserts without which they were impossible to play, but because of the first 45 I ever purchased, which I assumed was the theme from the short-lived and frankly racist cartoon *Hong Kong Phooey* but which turned out to be the short-lived and frankly racist disco anthem "Kung Fu Fighting."

The 8-Track Era (1973–1975)

For all the aspersions it has suffered, the 8-track remains a bellwether configuration. It is best understood as a pioneer technology in the incremental attempt by Americans to convert their automobiles into dwellings. Ashtrays. Bucket seats. Climate control. Why not a stereo?

My exposure to this innovation came via our babysitter Kay, who had a player in her Barracuda. On a few memorable occasions, when our parents needed to "unwind," Kay whisked us away for a weekend in Hollister, a town best known for its rather shortsighted nickname, *The Earthquake Capital of the World.* This meant the damp, doggy aroma of her apartment, shared with half a dozen Belgian sheepdogs, and a diet of A&W onion rings with the soggy onion removed.

How many nights did I lie curled in the back of the Barracuda as Kay cruised Route 25, Hollister's main drag, with Fleetwood Mac's "Rhiannon" pumping from her 8-track console? She took drags from her Parliaments and sang along—*She is like a cat in the dark, and then she is the darkness*—and the sheer gypsy longing of that song made me feel like a gypsy, mystical and exiled, and made me realize how sad Kay was, her voice rising through tendrils of blue smoke, her eyes bound in mascara and fixed on wherever she was going, which was where I was going too, which was nowhere.

The Cassette Era (1980–1991)

I can't remember exactly when cassettes displaced vinyl, but it happened quick and mean, like most everything else in the eighties, with a reflexive disdain for the relics of the past. Albums were clunky and lame, so 1979. Tapes were sci-fi marvels—an entire record that fit in your pocket. Then came boom boxes, which brought music into parks and abandoned homes and culverts, places where it was possible to smoke dope without having to exhale into a bottle of Brut cologne. You could carry a boom box on your shoulder. You could become a one-person mobile radio station with shitty reception and BO.

Then, about two seconds later, the Walkman appeared. One could now listen to music as a private activity in a public space. One could listen to the Cars' "Moving in Stereo" while actually *moving in stereo* through the main quad of your high school, in such a manner that regular people and objects assumed a sudden aqueous and symphonic significance, a discernible rhythm, and hitherto undetected emotional valences. Everyone became deeper and more beautiful.

We weren't just the stars of our videos. We were the directors, too. If we wanted the world to shimmer with exuberance, we played Katrina and the Waves ("Walking on Sunshine"). If we wanted to wallow in romantic suffering—and what adolescent doesn't?—we chose "Tempted" by Squeeze. If we wanted a dark jolt of aggression there was always Sabbath. Music, which had been a kind of world to which we applied, became something we applied to the world.

Cassettes could also be copied. The whippersnappers in the crowd, for whom the teat of piracy has come to feel like a birthright, will have trouble comprehending our dazzlement. Cassettes ran nine bucks retail back in 1983, or $2,700 in 2010 dollars. But you could buy blank tapes for forty-nine cents. So now we were into the production biz, too.

Inarguably, there were major drawbacks. To play a particular song required endless fast-forwarding and rewinding and declarations of "Okay, wait a second, dude, okay, here it is . . . shit, okay, just chill, it's right here. . . ." Tapes tended to melt in hot backseats, to warble in the presence of large, invisible magnets, to snap/tangle/unspool if you looked at them funny. I should mention the hiss, too, which grew increasingly prominent depending on the provenance of a tape. My copy of Prince's *Black Album*, for instance (bootlegged from a real live drug dealer!) included such classics as "Rockhard in a Hissy Place," "Superhissycalifragihissy," and, of course, "Let Me Stick My Big Hiss in U."

My loyalty to cassettes was inexplicable. I hated them. *Hated* them. But I had become a Fanatic at the dawn of the cassette era and soon had hundreds. I was, I'm fairly certain, the last music critic in

America requesting cassettes. "We don't really make tapes anymore," one flack told me. She paused. "Wait, were you joking?" I would still be listening to tapes, I suspect, had I not taken a new job and driven from El Paso to Miami in July of 1991. Half my collection melted on the trip down.

The CD Era (1992–2004)

I claim no romantic attachment to compact discs, nor can I explain in any reasonable fashion how I came to own four thousand of them. The crude math suggests I was acquiring one disc per day for these dozen years, with one day of rest per fortnight, a sort of Drooling Fanatic Sabbath. It's certainly true that my only consistent social activity was visiting used record shops. But now that I think about it, the reason I chose used record shops was because they accepted trade-ins, and I was trading in constantly, hauling dirty plastic sacks with shitty product someone else might want. So if we're being accurate, I've probably owned more like six thousand compact discs, or roughly 187 days of music. This figure is especially difficult to fathom, given that the job I took in Miami was as an investigative reporter.

Then again, I devoted far more time and imagination to the acquisition of CDs than to any of the jobs I held during this era. I lied to publicists more or less constantly. I trolled the dusty bins at Goodwill. I shoplifted. Even after quitting journalism and vowing never to return, I took a temporary position as a music editor to get myself back on the Music Industry Dole. Actually, I did this three times.

In 1997, I finally quit the papers for good and moved to Somerville to teach composition. It struck me as perfectly natural to demand that my students make me a mixed CD as part of their final exam. And to volunteer at my local NPR affiliate for the chance to pilfer the stacks of promo discs. I found an old Italian guy who built shelves and sold them out of his driveway. I ordered two CD shelves and two bookcases. Within a year, I had cleared the bookshelves to make room for CDs. Then I got the milk crates involved. Well, you know how this goes.

Did I make any effort to organize? Sort of. There was, for instance, a brief campaign to alphabetize. And a subsequent effort to organize by genre. For the most part, the CDs just piled up—on the coffee table, on the floor, on the windowsills. I had a small cache in the trunk of my car. Visitors were impressed by the size of the collection, though I could rarely find the particular CD I wanted them to hear. It might be said that my retentive compulsions had overrun my capacities for order. To quote my wife, upon her initial viewing of what I had described as my *music archive*: "Oh Jesus."

The Digital Era (2005–)

Knowing the dangers of a technological lag, I resolved to go digital the moment I heard about iTunes. First, though, I had to spend some time bitching about capitalism. This took five years. I then proceeded to the nearest Apple store and did my patriotic duty. iTunes was a revelation. Several tons of cumbersome recorded music could now be burned onto my hard drive, where it would be stored in perpetuity, available for play and distribution. I had gone from being a guy with CDs under his couch to a mid-size record company.

In those early days, I often fantasized about the truly epic library I was going to create, one that included not just my favorite albums but the one or two standout songs from the hundreds of mediocre records I owned, that would serve as a kind of distillate of my bloated collection. This library would be divided not by the dull and inadequate genre tags of the market, but by a more precise set of terms. *Pimp Soul* for Cee-Lo Green and Chuck Brown. *Ecstatic Rainy Day Stomp* for Phil Cody and Patrick Park. There'd be a whole section devoted to covers. And songs that mentioned candy. All tracks would be cross-referenced. There'd be a schematic tracing lines of influence, and a collateral filtering function. It was a beautiful vision, mathematical in its elegance.

Alas, my sloth. Transferring CDs to computer is not a particularly strenuous activity as compared with, say, harvesting potatoes. But it does require a degree of patience. There are decisions to be made. (Which albums to include? Which songs to include? How to classify and rate a particular song?) Heretofore, my collection had been predicated on *not* making such decisions. I was not so much a curator as a hoarder. To this day, less than 15 percent of my collection has made it onto the computer, and a good percentage of these songs are unidentifiable, because they were ripped from homemade discs and I was too "pressed for time" to type in the artist or track name. My own laziness saddens me.

But here's the thing: even if I had the energy to create such a library, I wouldn't have the room. I know this for a fact because my hard drive fried a couple of years back and I wound up paying a geek extortionist 1,300 smackers to get the thing running again, an operation that involved a new hard drive with "extra memory sticks" to accommodate the 8,500 songs in my library. And because my computer contains my entire creative life, I live in perpetual terror of doing anything to make it crash and so I'm terrified to add any more songs unless I remove an equivalent number, decisions over which I can easily fritter away, say, fourteen hours.

I assumed moving to a home three years ago would solve the storage crisis. Instead, owing to space issues associated with human breeding, my collection was stowed downstairs in what we call the Serial Killer Room, so called because it is dark and contains various menacing tools and stains on the concrete floor that are perhaps dried blood. The net effect of my digital revolution, in other words, is that I now have access to approximately a sixth of my collection.

The other eensy problem is how to play the music. In my old place,

I wound up rigging the computer to connect with my Bose boom box. In our new place, thanks to technological constraints far beyond my understanding, the Bose is no longer an option. So I wind up listening to music mostly on headphones plugged into my computer, or the computer speakers themselves, one of which recently blew. This is my fault, but I suspect there are a good number of you out there in the same bind. You've spent several thousand dollars to create an ultraconvenient digital library with the sound quality of a 1958 transistor radio.

To be clear: I don't begrudge the kiddies their jukeboxes the size of postage stamps, their boundless online troves. I'm thrilled to see the record companies properly fucked by the fans they've been fucking for years. I've rather enjoyed seeing musical equity return to its origins: live performance, those ancient rituals of collective listening.

Still, I can't help but view our sonic innovations as part of a massive techno-irony loop. Music has become more pervasive and portable than ever. But it feels less precious in the bargain. I don't want to confuse artistic and commercial value, but it's just a fact that some kid who rips an album for free isn't going to give it the same attention he would if it cost him ten bucks. At what point does convenience become spiritual indolence?

I realize this makes me sound like an old fart, but sometimes I get nostalgic for the days when the universe of recorded sound wasn't at our fingertips, when we had to hunt and wait and—horror of horrors—do without, when our longing for a particular record or song made it feel sacred. I miss the part of Fanaticism that involves unrequited longing, if that makes any sense.[5]

---

5. As I write this, it occurs to me that I've forgotten one configuration, the radio, which dominated my early childhood. I can remember listening to KFRC for hours, waiting for my favorite song to come on, and how ecstatic I was when the DJ finally played "The Things We Do for Love," or "Undercover Angel." Playing the records myself never felt as special. See, what I loved was that I'd surrendered to fate, which made the songs, when they finally arrived, feel like gifts.

List #3

Rock's Biggest Assholes

Compiled in the full knowledge that rock stars are paid to be assholes.

1. U2

Conceived of a concert tour mocking consumerism that was so grandiose and unimaginative it actually served as an advertisement for consumerism. At a show in Oslo, the quartet got trapped inside the giant mirrored lemon from which they were supposed to emerge. Tragically, they were rescued before they could eat each other.

2. Mick Jagger

Hey, Mick, how do you justify charging thousands of dollars for concert tickets? "It's super-competitive out there. There's a lot of tickets to move . . . It's capitalism. It's America. It's 2005."

   Oh.

3. Madonna

Responds to criticism of her devotion to Kabbalah by stating, "It would be less controversial if I joined the Nazi Party." I smell a career move!

4. The Beastie Boys

What's most obnoxious: that they dumped their original drummer because she didn't have a dick, that they appropriate the bankable parts of African-American culture, that they mock the rockers from whom they've stolen their best riffs, or that they now condemn misogyny after years of inspiring dudes to get trashed and paw women? I give up.

5. Pete Townshend

"I hope I die before I get old, or, at least, before I have to be propped up onstage and have large sticks attached to my arms so I can execute my trademark windmill guitar until such a time as my broker wires the proceeds directly to my dialysis machine."

6. Toby Keith

How to Get Rich, the Toby Keith Way:
- Respond to 9/11 by singing, "We'll put a boot in your ass/It's the American way."
- When asked six years later if you supported the Iraq War, respond, "Never did."
- Shill for Ford Trucks.
- Do a pro wrestling show.
- Remember not to laugh.

7. Kurt Cobain

Back in the early nineties Axl Rose twice asked Cobain if Nirvana would open for Guns N' Roses. Kurt responded by telling reporters how pathetic and untalented GNR was. It's hard to out-asshole Axl Rose, but you, dead sir, have done it!

8. Johnny Ramone

"Punk is right-wing."

9. Ted Nugent

George W. Bush once took the Nuge by the shoulders and said, "Just keep doing what you're doing." What action was the former president endorsing?

a) Introducing the phrase "wang dang sweet poontang" into the cultural lexicon
b) Shitting in Saddam Hussein's bidet
c) Suggesting an animal rights activist be clubbed like a baby harp seal
d) Failing to pay child support for a kid he's never met *and* taking legal custody of the seventeen-year-old girl he was bedding
e) Please don't make me think about either of these men

10. Scott Stapp

Jesus has agreed to forgive the former Creed singer his drug addiction, gun fetish, and domestic abuse if he stops making records.

5

What Songs Do

As a broad working definition, art awakens feeling. Every form has its merits and demerits. Paintings, for instance, work fast and require no moving parts, yet are hard to steal. Films are easy to watch and enveloping, but carry the risk you will see Philip Seymour Hoffman naked. The only thing wrong with music, as far as I'm concerned, is that you cannot eat it. From a purely emotional standpoint, it remains far more potent than any other artistic medium.

I remember the exact moment this dawned on me. I was watching *Late Night with David Letterman.* Willie Nelson was the guest. This was the watered-down Willie of the eighties, the stoner cowpoke in dusty pigtails. Dave was giving him a hard time. "Why don't you sing something for us?" Dave said, almost tauntingly. Willie sat there for a few seconds. And then he opened his mouth and began to sing and the sound of his voice—that glorious, battered baritone— sucked every bit of irony out of that room. Letterman looked stunned.

This is what songs do, even dumb pop songs: they remind us that emotions are not an inconvenient and vaguely embarrassing aspect of the human enterprise but its central purpose.[6] They make us feel specific things we might never have felt otherwise. Every time I listen to "Sunday Bloody Sunday," for instance, I feel a pugnacious righteousness about the fate of the Irish people. I hear that thwacking military drumbeat and Bono starts wailing about the news he heard today and I'm basically ready to enlist in the IRA and stomp some British Protestant Imperialist Ass, hell yes, bring on the fucking bangers and mash and let's get this McJihad started. I feel these things despite the fact that:

a. I am not Irish
b. The song actually advocates pacifism
c. I still wish U2 had eaten one another

The same thing happens with "Sweet Home Alabama." I don't exactly get psyched to join the Klan, but I do get this powerful desire to drink beer and drive a pickup truck and maybe shoot off some guns and most of all to not be looked down upon by some fucking overeducated, nigger-loving Yankee such as myself. Intellectually, I recognize that the song is shallow and racist, in that it advances the notion that former Alabama governor George Wallace—"I say segregation now, segregation tomorrow, segregation forever"—is an American hero. I also get that if all the members of Lynyrd Skynyrd were still alive, one or more of them would be members of the Republican

6. It might be said that Willie was, in his own way, introducing Letterman to a better version of himself. Then again, one of the things I hope this book will *not* do is traffic in the seductive myth that music morally improves people. It certainly uncorks volatile feelings that would otherwise remain bottled up, which, I would argue, generally improves people's lives. But there's no way to establish whether this counts as a net positive for the species. If we're going to give hymns credit for saving the sinner we'll also have to blame Wagner for psyching up a bunch of Nazis, and we'll have to take seriously the claims that heavy metal and hip-hop act as accessories in the commission of certain crimes, and we'll have to think about what it means that so many young soldiers use music to whip themselves into a killing mood. No thanks.

congressional leadership team. But I can't help it: "Sweet Home Alabama" makes me feel a deep yearning for my home and my kin and
the swampers in Muscle Shoals who pick me up when I'm feeling
blue, even though these same swampers would possibly kick my Jew
ass sideways if I ever sidled into one of their taverns and ordered me
a Chablis.

Songs take us deeper into ourselves by taking us away from ourselves. They expand our empathic imaginations. When we listen to "I
Will Survive" by Gloria Gaynor we become empowered sisters show-
ing our abusive exes the door, and when we listen to "Rocket Man" (or
maybe, in your case, "Space Oddity") we become astronauts blasted
away from our loved ones into orbits of lonely obligation, and when
we listen to "Jack & Diane" we become teenagers sucking on chili
dogs and reveling in the fleeting ecstasies of green love. And God
knows, we're all homesick travelers when we hear "Homeward
Bound," *even when we're at home.*

I've cherry-picked songs that most people know. But like any other
Fanatic I've got an endless list of obscure songs that induce the same
kind of weirdly gratifying identity crisis. "When I Was Drinking" by
the band Hem makes me want to be an alcoholic. It makes me want
to be an alcoholic involved with another alcoholic. It makes me pine
for the perverse safety of all the self-defeating relationships I've ever
been in. That's how beautiful that fucking song is. (I'm fairly sure the
heroine of "When I Was Drinking" used to date the guy in the
Replacements' "Here Comes a Regular," though the songs were
released two decades apart.) "Taj Mahal" by the Canadian band Sam
Roberts has a nearly opposite effect. I listen to this organ-drenched
ode and feel a completely unwarranted sense that love is a form of
destiny impervious to time. "Listen Here" by Eddie Harris makes me
so mellow I briefly become Buddhist.

When people complain about how crappy most commercial pop
music is, what they're really angry about is that particular songs don't

take them anywhere. We may have some kind of involuntary limbic reaction to the tune and beat, but they stall out as emotional transport devices. Sometimes, this is because the listener is unwilling to give the song a chance. But often, it's a matter of the aesthetic choices that have been made. They're too easy, too obvious in their desire to manipulate our feelings.

I am thinking (without quite wanting to) of Debby Boone's "You Light Up My Life," a song I was forced to sing in my fifth-grade chorus and which I necessarily repudiated with many retching sounds in public, but which I also privately adored, often staring out the window of the room I shared with my brothers and softly imitating Debby's dewy vibrato, even tearing up as she soared toward the climactic line, *It can't be wrong when it feels so right.* The song was all I thought about for several months. It inflamed my desires. I wanted to devote myself to Christ and feel up Debby Boone, ideally at the same time. And then, just as suddenly, I began to hate the song, its sappy lyrics and synthesized strings, the confused yearning it revealed in me.

We all do this, of course. We develop brief, blinding crushes on songs like "You Light Up My Life" (or "Candle in the Wind" or "Say You, Say Me"[7] or "Wake Me Up Before You Go-Go"). Then those crushes end and the musical artifacts we took to be genuinely inspiring and heartfelt and even redemptive reveal themselves as repetitive and crass, a kind of emotional propaganda, and we feel like suckers.

No Depression—or, Actually, Check That, Fuckloads of Depression

And that's fine. That's *okay.* For the Drooling Fanatic, life is littered with these vulgar infatuations, because of our sensitivity to the dra-

---

7. To those of you who will now accuse me of picking on Lionel Richie because of my brief and disastrous sexual relationship with his daughter, let me assure you that "Easy" remains one of my favorite songs on earth, a track that has made that mysterious journey from the Valley of Utter Cheese to the Kingdom of Total Coolness.

matic capacities of music. We're ready to fall in love, one song at a time. This is something I failed to note earlier, when I was talking about the pedigree of our breed. And it's maybe the most important indicator of DF tendencies, which is that *we're chronically emotional people who have trouble accessing our emotions.*

In my own case—though I suspect this is broadly true—repression was our family religion. I didn't admit to anyone else that I was feeling sad or frightened or angry because I saw little hope of being regarded or soothed, and a good chance of being mocked. And so I started to hide these feelings from myself; they burrowed inward and took cover under a sarcastic bravado. When I wanted to numb myself out, I watched TV. But songs had the opposite effect. They became a secret passageway to emotion, a way of locating what I was feeling before I entirely understood it myself.

The earliest example I can offer takes place in the summer of 1971, when, at age four, my twin brother and I were transplanted from the suburbs to a commune in the rolling hills of Ukiah.[8] My folks were hoping for a rural utopia. What they found was an unsupervised summer camp. The tenor of those feverish months is best captured by the episode in which a man known as Big John wound up dropping acid, then climbing into the bathtub with Mike and me, despite being fully clothed. More than any particular moment, though, what I remember of that place is the song "American Pie," which was always playing and to which people were always singing along. I didn't understand certain words—What was a levee? How could one drink rye?—but I got that it was a story about saying good-bye to something lovely and doomed. It was the moment, so common in American social movements, when a dispiriting present gives way to nostalgia. There must have been other songs playing (this was 1971 after all) but I was four

---

8. I'm discounting an earlier episode, in which my mother sang "I Want to Hold Your Hand" to me and I reached out for her, because I was at the time eleven months old.

years old and this was the one I needed to make sense of what was happening around me.

I've always been drawn to songs that make me feel bad and that make feeling bad feel good. These songs—Depression Songs—allow us to slough the small emotions that compose our defense mechanisms for the large emotions that make us feel genuinely alive. They convert self-pity into sorrow, anxiety into fear, grievance into grief.

To clarify: Depression Songs don't make people depressed. They articulate a preexisting depression and, when they're really cooking, they *ennoble* that depression. They offer tremendous relief to those of us otherwise prone to wallowing. Nearly all the songs I return to, the ones that have come to represent entire eras of my life, are Depression Songs. Everybody has his or her own set list, because the main ingredient in the construction of a Depression Song is you, the depressed listener.

If you play the song "Nothing Compares 2 U" by Sinéad O'Connor, for instance, my wife is instantly transported back to 1990, managing the cosmetics section at CVS, a shy fifteen-year-old mooning over one in a series of mulleted cads to whom she had pledged undying love. It's all there: the knot in her throat, the heavy bands of blue eye shadow, the mocking promises on the glass bottles of nail polish it was her job to shelve.

My time-equivalent Depression Song—I confess this with little pride—is "Never Tear Us Apart" by INXS, which you might remember as the one with the video where the comely lead singer Michael Hutchence wanders morosely around Prague and then, right at the end, accidentally hangs himself while masturbating. It's an addictive soul song built around synths, a quartet of plucked guitar notes, and various dramatic pauses. The vocals are overwrought in the best way. Hutchence tells his lover that they could live for "a thousand years/But if I hurt you I make wine from your tears," and rather than questioning how that would work, or how such a wine might taste, or what, exactly, it would mean that you might want to use the tears of your lover to make an alcoholic beverage, my intuitive reaction is to think, That is just *heavy*. This was certainly what I was thinking as I staggered across the soggy lawns of my college campus, having just enjoyed a one-night stand that I assumed would last for a thousand years and produce oceans of Chardonnay. My inamorata had a slightly different take. She cringed when she saw me the next day. We were not going to last a thousand years. We had barely lasted a thousand seconds.

And then there's the song "Hello, Mary" by David Baerwald. The melody alone is enough to put me on a crying jag, but the part that slays me is three minutes in, when the hero, who's been talking to an old lover, trying to play things cool, suddenly blurts out, "I was looking at a picture, it was me and you, I think it was 1982, and you were sitting on my lap and my hand was on your breast and we were staring into each other's eyes" and on this last word his voice rises into a helpless falsetto and you realize that, though he's not in love with her, he's still in love with that moment of loving her and he'll never be rid of that feeling. That I was obsessed with "Hello, Mary" throughout my first failed love affair did not dawn on me as significant. I was twenty-one years old.

As for "We've Never Met" by Neko Case, I can't listen to that one without drowning in the anguish of my first year in Boston, getting dumped by women who were only doing what I asked them to do, which is why I listen to it *all the time*. That weepy steel guitar and Neko's velvety alto and Ron Sexsmith's whispered harmonies. It sounds exactly like what I always wish Patsy Cline will sound like, but never does. *You were golden and I was blind, now it's like we've never met.* I have yet to find a better definition of unrequited love.

All the Lonely People

These examples all derive from the predominant genre of Depression Songs, the Heartbreak Song, to which we might add several thousand without much effort, including "Tired of Being Alone" by Al Green, "The Sun Is Gonna Shine" by Aretha, and "It's All Over Now, Baby Blue." Have I forgotten one? Oh yes, "Missing You" by John Waite.

Not every Heartbreak Song is a Depression Song. "Song for the Dumped" by Ben Folds offers the exuberant refrain, "Give me my money back, you bitch." It's not designed to bum us out, but to make us laugh (a bit ruefully) at the rage we throw in the face of rejection.

Depression Songs actually work better when they're about something other than depression. This is why "Eleanor Rigby" is so much more compelling than "Yesterday." Paul McCartney found a story, with actual characters who were able to personify a condition of solitude, whereas "Yesterday" is really just Paul whining.

"Eleanor Rigby" also has a more ambitious arrangement. George Martin recognized the song's symphonic possibilities: the constricted moan of those strings, the rueful countermelody of the cellos, the squall of the single violin that trembles across the chorus. These decisions don't just contribute to the mood of collective isolation; they *are* the mood.

On the other hand, one of the best Depression Songs of recent years, "Down the Line" by José González (an Argentine based, confusingly, in Sweden), includes nothing more than a voice, a couple of guitars, and a drum loop. González has a delicate voice, and he seems to be addressing a friend about an impending breakdown. But he chops at his guitar with a nervous urgency, and the melody keeps struggling against its own foreboding. "Don't let the darkness eat you up," González sings over and over at the end of the song, and you want to believe his pal is going to be all right but you also know, without wanting to, that he's not, and that González knows he's not. It's a song about trying to save the unsavable, and it about ruins me every time I hear it.

On the other side of the coin is "Dance Music" by the Mountain

Goats. The song is two minutes long, with a peppy piano riff. It's the kind of ditty that would make Trent Reznor break out in hives. But it's actually way sadder than anything Reznor has ever written because John Darnielle, the singer, has the guts to reveal the tragedies of his life without hiding behind enraged slogans. He recounts a scene in which his stepfather throws a glass at his mother's head. Darnielle then dashes upstairs and leans in close to the record player on the floor. "So this is what the volume knob's for," he sings. "I listen to dance music." It's a Depression Song about why people need happy music.

Reluctant Exegesis:
"Fade to Black"

This section started out as a lengthy riff mocking the lyrical shortcomings of Metallica, as well as depressed teenagers who play Dungeons and Dragons. This is pretty asinine behavior, in particular when you happen to be married to an ex-D&D geek who, at sixteen, learned the entire lead guitar part (solos included) to "Fade to Black."

I wasn't aware of this last fact, because my wife avoids talking about her teenage years. It's a painful subject even now, though I didn't realize how painful until she read my lame exegesis and began to talk about what "Fade to Black" had meant to her.

So let's travel back to East Hartford, Connecticut, circa 1986. Erin is twelve years old, a shy sixth grader at St. Christopher's. Like most budding DFs, she lives in the thrall of an older sibling, in this case Rob, two years her senior, handsome and popular and unruly, a badass with big hair. One day, Rob plays her a tape of a band called Poison. The album cover confuses her—are the members women or men?—but the music slices through her like lightning. Before long, she's moved on to the heavy stuff—Anthrax, Megadeth, Metallica. Posters go up on her wall. Her hair rises skyward in a fusillade.

Her parents, strict Catholics, are aghast. Erin has always been the good one, studious, pliant, the kind of kid who memorizes the lives of the saints. Her mother has developed the sweetly deranged fantasy that her daughter will someday play violin for the Hartford Symphony. Erin's announcement that she is quitting violin to take up electric guitar serves as a formal declaration of war. Her father is dispatched upstairs to tear the posters from her walls, to confiscate all records deemed offending and redact the rest. Her mother will later carry a tape of Mötley Crüe's *Shout at the Devil* into the backyard and smash it to bits with a hammer.

The mistakes are easy enough to see in retrospect. If one were writing a manual entitled "How to Ensure That Your Troubled Teen Will Fall into the Clutches of Heavy Metal," Erin's folks provide a useful model. But their sense of betrayal is honest and not without sympathy. Heavy metal is telling them everything they don't want to know about their daughter: that she is angry, that she is a sexual being, and (most painfully) that she dreams of escape. What parent wants to be told such things?

In ninth grade, Erin transitions into public high school. She hangs out with the bad kids, her brother's friends especially. Having grown up amid the obsessive sexual prohibitions of the Church, she now saunters the neighborhood in stretch jeans for the sheer pleasure of hearing men in cars honk at her. Her parents are convinced she has become a fallen woman, though she is in fact that far more common breed among metal chicks: a virgin seeking the power of a slut.

It is amid this feuding that Erin finds "Fade to Black." Most metal songs are aspirational, wishful odes to hedonism. "Fade to Black" is a dirge about a guy so alienated he savors the prospect of his own suicide. The song strikes Erin as an epic transcription of her life. She, too, feels hopelessly misunderstood, trapped with no way out. For months, she's been scouring the want ads for rented rooms. But she has no money and no way to get a job.

She listens to "Fade to Black" over and over: the somber opening notes, the chords ringing out above the martial thump. She learns it on the guitar because she wants to be noticed by the older boys, and because she figures maybe she'd become a rock star and that will be her ticket out. She likes the ending best, after James Hetfield growls *"Death greets me warm, now I will just say goodbye"* and Kirk Hammett rips into his solo and the whole band starts to gallop, triumphant, unstoppable, a violent blur. She knows it's fucked up that "Fade to Black" makes suicide heroic, but that's how it feels, like she'll be seizing control of her life once and for all, meting out the ultimate punishment to her parents.

Things get worse. They always do in this kind of story. Rob moves out of the house and the disputes between Erin and her folks escalate into physical altercations. One afternoon, she is pulled out of class by her parents and driven to a psychiatric hospital. Their goal is naïve, if not quite unkind. They want professionals to take away the wild mascaraed creature that dwells upstairs and return to them the docile, straight-A student they can safely love. They are genuinely shocked when the doctors suggest family counseling. Soon after, Erin arrives at school with an injured finger. The school nurse asks her what happened; she bursts into tears. This is when the social workers get involved.

At sixteen, Erin moves into a friend's basement. She hangs out with the metal chicks at school and cuts classes. She forms a band (The Virgin Saints) and finds a boy happy to relieve her of her virginity. Late at night, in her basement room, she writes poetry. She doesn't want for ambition. It's guidance she needs.

Sometimes, Erin still wonders how her life might have been different if she'd had some amazing teacher who put the right book in her hands. It's an understandable wish. But she didn't have that kind of fortune. What she had was "Fade to Black," which, for all its bombast, offered the essential lesson: that it was her job to document the unbearable feelings, to convert the bruisings of her heart into beauty.

Am I now suggesting that I find "Fade to Black" beautiful? Yes, I suppose I am. Or maybe I'm suggesting, more plausibly, that I love my wife and all she's struggled against to become who she is and that "Fade to Black" is an indispensable part of that.

And let me add, as a crucial coda, that what makes "Fade to Black" so easy to tease is, upon further examination, what makes it so affecting. The lyrics sound *exactly* like the poems Erin was scrawling in her basement lair. The nature of adolescence, after all, forces upon us two conflicting desires: to confess everything, every mutilated impulse and bloated woe, while, at the same time, suppressing all incriminating evidence. The solution (as recorded in every teenage journal ever written, as affirmed at every heavy metal concert ever staged) is to encode these feelings and their explicit causes in abstract and overwrought couplets. It is this same impulse that drives the bravest among us from language into the cleansing howl of rock and roll.

In Erin's case, though, she headed in the other direction. Like me, she eventually recognized the limits of her talent. And though she was for a time, no doubt about it, the best female heavy metal guitar player in central Connecticut, it was her devotion to words that got her to community college, then on to college, and graduate school. She found that larger life, beyond the reach of her parents, whom she loves now with great patience, from a safe distance. Like me, they will never truly understand what "Fade to Black" means, or how many Erins it has saved from self-annihilation.

6

Nil Lara Was Our Messiah

There was a big bunch of us back then in Miami, all in our twenties, eager and horny and half-formed, if that. There were only three things we knew for sure. We knew South Beach was blowing up. We knew greatness awaited us. And we knew Nil Lara was going to be the most famous musician on earth.

Every other week we gathered at a club called the Stephen Talkhouse on Washington Avenue, two blocks from the glittering neglected sea, to watch Nil and his band destroy pop music as we knew it, as something discrete and classifiable and safely secular. The place smelled of lemon rinds and Marlboro Lights and we drank the sweet drinks of our twenties and huddled close to flirt. Nil never started on time. If handbills said DOORS AT NINE, you were unwise to expect a note until eleven, though he did two sets, always. If you got out of there before three in the morning it was only because you were sick in spirit. Most of us worked at the *Miami New Times*, the alternative fishwrap, and you could always tell the morning after a weekday show, the smoke and beer stench rinsed but not ridden, the bluish dabs of missing sleep beneath our eyes, a dreamy ringing in our ears.

"Nil?" someone would say.

And we'd say, "Yeah, Nil."

We'd say it like we were speaking the name of a lover because we were in love with Nil, all of us, in love with his voice and the way he flicked at his guitar and the moony hopes that surged through us when he had his band at full pace. There was one night in particular (whenever it was) an hour into his second set and he was playing "Mama's Chant," howling an Afro-Cuban incantation while we twirled beneath him, and he reached the bridge and passed the valley of solos and led his band into that bright clearing where the song itself exploded into something larger, a mood of cheerful chaos, the tiny dance floor being ectoplasm at this point, with all the usual suspects sloshing away—Lenny the Large and Tilson and beautiful Paloma and Floodie and yours truly, known in those days as The Spoon—and the old *conguero*, Baro, in a metronomic trance and Nil moving also, thumping his bare feet between the amp cables and, at some invisible cue, directing his keyboardist to play a familiar bubbling run of notes, at which point Nil burst out, "Very superstitious, writing's on the wall," so that for the next three minutes we were all Stevie Wonder, we were all blind black singers, exalted, swollen and nodding, even if Nil was the only one whose high sweet baritone could grant the notes their proper due, the only one who could gently bend the room back toward his song, which we figured would end the jam, would leave us all in a happy ruined heap of vodka fumes except that Nil began a high-kneed march and the bassist came in with a low drubbing and the drummer snapped at his kit and the guitarist (a towering shredder, a ferocious spider) nodded and came down hard on the chords instantly recognizable to anyone alive during the long slow death of prog rock. . . .

We don't need no education!
We don't need no thought control!

And this was the holy shit of all holy shits, the moment when every single person in the Talkhouse (right down to the brooding bartender) felt the delicious howl of high school—the endless fascism of parents and teachers and The Man—come roaring out of our throats, like *we* were bricks, man, like *we* were the ones marching into the meat grinder and getting our soft hearts cranked into ground chuck; we didn't even look around, we didn't do anything but scream and scream and dance and scream and Nil got a frank look of pleasure on his face and shook his head because without meaning to he'd led us all back to the garage where fifteen years earlier he had played these exact notes and sung these exact words and dreamed of this exact moment, of a hundred souls ready to join his crusade and carry his banner into the world. These were the times when we knew Nil couldn't miss, that it was only a matter of time until the world snatched him up and away from us, which made us a little sad but also chosen, which made us want to kneel before him, touch the hem of his garment, which sent us staggering out onto the damp sidewalks trembling with gratitude.

Enter the Spoon

It's like this when you fall hard for a musician. It's a crush with religious overtones. You listen to the songs and you memorize the words and the notes and this is a form of prayer. You attend the shows and this is the liturgy. You're interested in relics—guitar picks, set lists, the sweaty napkin applied to His brow. You set up shrines in your room. It's not just about the music. It's about who you are when you listen to the music and who you wish to be and the way a particular song can bridge that gap, can make you feel the abrupt thrill of absolute faith.

For which we were all searching back then, being young and subject to the Drooling Fanatical hopes of youth. We felt we were part of something larger. Why not? We were living in Miami Beach, watching the place transform before our eyes from a beachfront slum to a tattooed Riviera, the old Jews and the dope fiends and the deranged mumblers quietly nudged out to make room for Gianni Versace and Bobby De Niro and the parade of models who sunned themselves topless on the patch of beach around Fourteenth Street, watching the old palaces of the Art Deco district gutted, replenished, repainted in cake frosting colors, their nautical railings and porthole windows buffed to a gleam, made seaworthy again. The wood floors of my studio, at the corner of Meridian and Tenth, were forever dusted with sand.

This was back in 1991 and it wasn't much later that I heard Nil for the first time, in a club called the Spot. I don't remember anything else about the occasion (who I was with for instance), only that Nil was flicking at a tiny Cuban guitar called a *tres* and singing. He was too talented for the Spot, which was the kind of place where people came to do eight balls in the bathroom and get their photos in the social pages of local rags like the one where I worked. His songs had a melodic purity that could have derived only from the Beatles—you hummed them, they hummed you—but delivered in a style that incorporated the crooked rhythms of Cuban *son* and the stately phrasing of the *canción*, that struck the ear as both savage and exquisitely controlled, and he did this (mind you) with a three-piece.

I stood there screaming *Who is this guy?* and *Dude, are you guys hearing this?* and all the other things DFs scream, until my friends toddled off to the next bar and I was left standing about three feet from Nil, clapping too loud. I accosted him after his set and he handed me a vinyl copy of an album by his old band KRU, which I clutched to my chest like a teenybopper.

It took another year for Nil to put his band together and move to the Talkhouse. The crowds were small at first, mostly folks me and Floodie dragged from work. A nervous energy permeated the room the moment Nil began. We knew what our bodies wanted and Nil certainly knew, but we were also frightened, being essentially suburban middle-class strivers who spent our days behaving in a manner meant to avoid embarrassment. This battle would rage inside each of us until someone worked up the nerve to start dancing, at which point everyone poured out of their seats.

This was the era during which I came to be called The Spoon, the nickname deriving from a pair of boots I'd bought used on Washington Avenue, stupendously ugly boots by any measure, fashioned in the cowboy style but cut off just above the ankle, as if the cobbler had run short on black leather and panicked. On the plus side, the slick wooden heel made a loud clacking when stomped on the floor—like someone playing the spoons. It would be nice to suppose I was given this nickname as a tribute to my percussive sangfroid. I certainly felt nimble. I had moves: the stomp, the sudden controlled skid, the splayfooted pelvis hop, the booty bop, the shoulder juke. It was during this era that I broke a woman's foot on the dance floor at a Polish wedding in Toledo, Ohio, which should serve as the best and most disturbing testament to the delusions of grace I suffered during Nil's reign. But we all felt like that. We all danced like that. We all believed he had been sent to liberate our secret wishes.

Into the Mystic

If this sounds grandiose, consider the larger messianic context. Miami was being touted as America's designated City of Destiny, its ultraglamorous melting pot. This was partly civic marketing crapola, but it was also true that you couldn't swing a dead cat without hitting a new cultural enclave and everyone seemed to know someone who knew an actual Santeria priest or a *curandera* or a Haitian dude who did voodoo part-time. Nil was our polyglot poster boy. The guy had mastered all the standard rock idioms *and* immersed himself in the roots music of the Caribbean and South America. He played fifteen different instruments, half of his own invention. He dressed in billowing smocks and torn trousers—half crooner, half Caliban.

Nil also cultivated that trait so essential to rock stars: mystery. We knew next to nothing about him and swapped rumors constantly. He lived alone with a monkey. Gloria Estefan had propositioned him. He had grown up in the Amazon jungle. No, he came from Cuba on a raft. He was a *balsero*. That he was born in Newark and later moved to Venezuela (facts we would eventually unearth) hardly mattered.

Major label execs soon began turning up at the Talkhouse. David Byrne himself flew down from New York City to do his best geek schmooze. What a strange pleasure, to see those suits squeezed in at the edges of the bar. Nil could have moved to a bigger venue, but he enjoyed the heat of our packed bodies.

Nil was our soundtrack, after all. His music expressed the hopes we felt as we churned reluctantly toward adulthood. I was growing into an intrepid journalist. Every six weeks, my name appeared on the cover of our paper and I strutted around like that meant something. Floodie and me became best friends. We'd get stoned and hit the grimy juice bar on Washington Avenue and head down to the beach and thrash out to the buoy and do pull-ups until our tits ached. Floodie taught me how to run, too, on the boardwalk that began at Seventeenth, dodging Hassids and leathery vagrants, Floodie moving like a gazelle while I staggered behind cursing. We were in love, though we wouldn't have seen it that way. And just to make sure, I went goony for Paloma, the ad rat in the next cubicle. She was a Miami native, gorgeous, Cuban, with a clever violent family and complicated underwear. One night, after months of awkward courting, after tequila and Nil, she let me walk her to her car. I was a stuttering wreck.

"Relax," she said, "I'm coming back to your place."

Which she did and (by the way) bedded me with a nonchalance I found terrifying. I woke up a few hours later with the absolute conviction that my life had arrived. On weekends, we repaired to her house in Westchester and ate cheap Chinese and frozen yogurt and rented videos. Weeknights, I returned to my place on South Beach and worked on short stories. Nil was a part of all this. Watching him made me impatient for the change I could feel within myself. My imagination was puny and obvious, but I was reaching toward the feelings that would turn out to matter.

For the sake of proper plotting, I managed to convince myself that Paloma and Nil were sneaking around behind my back. This was a fantasy mostly about Nil, I suspect. And there was of course that one night when I came upon the two of them huddled at the bar. I spent the rest of the weekend fuming. But I never confronted Paloma. And the next week I was back at the Talkhouse, dancing in my ugly boots.

Shine, Even for a While

The scene always falls apart, though never how you think it will. We kept expecting Nil to get whisked away on a magic carpet of fame. Instead, the Talkhouse shut down. South Beach had become the sort of terrain where foam parties[9] drew more paying customers than Richard Thompson.

Nil's last gig there was April 16, 1995, a Sunday. I kept a flyer tucked away for years, though I don't remember the show itself, only the ringing after-moments, our sore feet, our raw throats, the purple hint of dawn. The music was over. It didn't take long for us to kill our own happiness.

Paloma and I began to drift into the brainless grievances that signal erotic demise. We decided drugs might help and one night resorted to a candyflip—half acid and half Ecstasy. The pills sickened

---

9. You are to be forgiven if you don't recall the heyday of the foam party. It was a European fad in which the dance floor of a club—usually a gay club—was flooded with soap bubbles, allowing revelers to pleasure one another under cover of suds.

us. She lay down on my bed and moaned while I stumbled outside and tried to walk it off. Before long, I stood amid the hordes of Ocean Drive, lobster-colored tourists, models and muscle boys and pimps and playgirls, all frolicking in puddles of neon, reeking of suntan lotion and clove cigarettes and puke. They sent shots gurgling down their throats and plucked buttery morsels from oversize plates, everyone on the make for pleasures they didn't quite deserve. This was Bosch by way of the tropics. And it was perhaps at this moment that I fell out of love with Miami Beach itself and came to see the place as a monument to self-regard, though probably it was half an hour later, having staggered naked into the rancid Atlantic and emerged to find nothing changed.

Then Floodie lost his mind. He was a supremely gentle soul—a loyal Deadhead even—but the chemicals inside him had their own agenda. He threatened to assault his boss, took up with cocaine, and disappeared for days at a time, returning with the fervent assurances of the mad. I went to visit him one night and walked straight into a NO PARKING sign, the edge of which caught my brow and opened a bloody gash. That's how I seemed to be doing.

Paloma never took up with Nil, so far as I discovered. Instead, she succumbed to the entreaties of her girlfriend Bella, with whom she necked passionately in a bar, either on top of or near a pool table depending on whom you believed. Within a few months, she'd left town and I'd taken up with a histrionic intern, an act of loneliness I mistook for revenge. Nil wasn't to blame for any of this. But we couldn't help feeling that the end of his run at the Talkhouse was the end of us, too, of that peculiar era in which our dreams cancel out all our mistakes.

Nil released his debut on Capitol Records in March of 1996. Jon Pareles of *The New York Times* hailed the album as a masterpiece and Nil launched his long-awaited national tour. I kept waiting to see him on TV, serenading Rachel from *Friends*. But when I saw Nil again it was at a tiny club in Winston-Salem, North Carolina. He looked thin and drawn and had a cast on his foot.

I saw him only once more, in Miami, where I'd returned from grad school, hoping to recapture those fruity vapors of youth. Floodie came with me, though he was married now, a skittish adult with a kid and a mortgage. The crowd was young, club kids mostly, waiting for the DJ to show up and christen their drug trips. They didn't seem to know who Nil was, or why he mattered, and when I tried to revive the Spoon they looked at me like I was an old dog performing a sad trick. Then I dropped my beer and everything got fucked up beyond repair. After the set I hugged Nil and he hugged me back, though I didn't understand what was happening exactly; that we were saying farewell. Nil didn't release another album for eight years.

Barbaric Expressions of the Soul

I figured this would be a sad story, because my own head is stuffed with foolish notions about what it means to succeed as an artist. But that's not how this story ends. Nor does it end with some squalid meeting in South Beach—Nil guzzling yage tea and babbling about how he could have been a contender. It ends with a brief, polite phone conversation.

I asked Nil what he was up to these days. He gets that question a lot. His website message board is full of DFs like me, still waiting for him to conquer the world. "I'll play out maybe once a month," he said, "make it an event. I get a lot of younger musicians. Every few shows, some kid'll come up to me with all these questions about the music industry and the next thing I know he's selling a million records." Nil laughed. "I did the major-label thing. I put my two cents out there for people to discover and now I'm traveling below the radar. I don't mind. It's kind of cool actually."

He sounded astonishingly unbitter about his relationship with

Capitol. "It was the ride of a lifetime," Nil said. "How could it not be awesome? I got to travel around the whole country, twice. I got over to Europe. I met a ton of cool people. I was bringing the Talkhouse to the rest of the world."

But didn't he have *any* regrets? Nil paused for a second. "I wish I would have had a better sense of myself, and stopped touring after a year. But, you know, the label said, 'Keep touring, keep touring,' and I figured they must know something I don't. Two years of sleeping in a van, getting up at five a.m., doing the radio, the in-stores, then a show, you know, my body just crashed."

By the time Nil brought Capitol a follow-up, the folks who had signed him were long gone. He and the label agreed to part ways. In 2004, Nil put out two records on his own, which you can still find online if you hunt. These days, he sticks with the live shows. "You sell fifteen, twenty records. No middleman, just cash in your pocket."

I told Nil about the night he'd given me a KRU record, so long ago.

"I don't remember that, but I remember you at the Talkhouse, man. Dancing and dancing and dancing. Bouncing Steve. You'd come up to me after a show and hug me and you were covered with sweat. That I remember."

I apologized, retrospectively.

"That's cool," he said. "That's what it's all about, man. Barbaric expressions of the soul."

I was struck by the precision of the term, by Nil's lyrical talents in general, something I've neglected to emphasize. The guy had a sick sense of rhythm, a melodic knack to rival McCartney, a voice of uncommon range and clarity. But he also wrote beautifully in two languages, three if you include the Afro-Cuban scat he did when the spirit took him. It made me suddenly furious again on Nil's behalf. "Doesn't it even bug you, though," I said, "to know you never got what you deserved?"

There was another pause. I hoped I'd maybe knocked some of the poise out of Nil.

"That's okay," he said softly. "Be selfish. Keep it to yourself."

His voice was full of tenderness; I felt a lump in my throat. Was I going to weep? Was Nil Lara going to make me weep after all these years? "What does 'big' mean, anyway?" he said. "That I get to go play in a mall? Or some giant arena where everything's lit up and you can't see anyone? I've played in those places, Steve. It's like you're in a vacuum. No, I like bars. You order a beer and there's a band and that's it. You can see the faces, the bodies dancing. What else could I want?"

Nil was saying, in essence: those nights of song at the Talkhouse— they *were* the dream. The rest was just the ambition we'd gathered on his behalf, which he was returning to me now, gently, without a hint of anger. I wanted to tell Nil that he was my hero, that he'd inspired me to become more than I thought I could. But I knew that would sound hokey, so I told him I should let him go and hung up and ran down to the basement and found his first record and blasted the thing and tried to remember the last time I'd felt so full of hope.

Interlude:
Five Really Stupid Things I've Done as a Drooling Fanatic

1. Serving as an X-Rated DJ to 200 Small Jewish Children The summer after my freshman year in college, I was hired as a counselor at Camp Tova. This was a very bad decision for all involved. I lacked certain counseling essentials, such as a fondness for six-year-olds and any sense of the activities they might enjoy. "Let's do some weight training!" I might say. Or, "Who wants to visit the cemetery?"

The crucial thing was this: the arts and crafts counselor was *hot*. She was five years older than me and she went to arts school in New York City and knew actual junkies. To impress her, I volunteered to DJ the first (and only) camp dance party and spent the next three weeks fretting over the playlist. The big day arrived. The children filed into the multipurpose room. Overweening Jewish mothers assembled to chaperone. The Camp Director gestured for the music to begin.

Was it wise for me to open with "Psycho Killer" by Talking Heads? I will say no. Nor was "Shout" by Tears for Fears especially apt. Then I played "Add It Up" by the Violent Femmes, which begins with Gordon Gano wailing, *Why can't I get just one kiss?* It's an energetic anthem of lust, which I spent energetically lusting after the arts and crafts babe, who was dancing with a bunch of kids (lustily if you must know the truth). Did the ethical concerns of playing such a song for six-year-olds occur to me? Not really. I was more occupied by its effects on the arts and crafts babe and how she might be induced to grant me *just one fuck*. And why did this phrase leap to mind? Because, come to think of it, Gordon Gano was just about to wail it to an auditorium full of six-year-olds and their Jewish mothers and the Camp Director.

I turned from the dance floor and began a slow-motion dash toward my record player, because this was still a situation I could rescue, I could break the kids into two groups for a quick game of Sharks and Minnows, or Who Wants to Not Report the DJ to Child Protective Services? But Gano was singing too fast and I was too far away and the Camp Director was staring at me with her mouth open. Then I plowed into one of my campers, a lethargic little turd named Corey who continually farted during story hour. It was this collision that doomed me, because you can't run over a six-year-old and keep going, though believe me I considered it, and thus, as I pulled him upright and brushed him off, I heard Gano's anguished contralto ask the assembled,

> *Why can't I get just one fuck?*
> *I guess it's something to do with luck*

Actually, it's not.

2. Agreeing to Buy James Cotton Medicine This dates back to my days as a rock critic in El Paso, though the show in question took place 350 miles away, in Lubbock. I had managed to convince my editor that James Cotton was one of the most important musicians on earth and close to dying. The former was possibly true, if you consider harmonica the most important instrument on earth. The latter I made up. The reason I wanted to interview Cotton was that my pal Holden had just been shipped off to Lubbock.

I showed up early for the concert and found his road manager, who led me backstage. As a younger man, Cotton had fronted Howlin' Wolf's band and toured with Janis Joplin and done backflips on stage. He was well past his acrobatic days. He moved slowly; his hands trembled.

"You gonna be all right?" his manager said.

Cotton nodded.

Once his manager was gone Cotton turned and, as if noticing me for the first time, said, "You suppose you could do me a favor, young man?"

"Of course," I said.

"I need to get some medicine."

"Sure," I said.

This would make awesome color for my story. What could be better than fetching medicine for a dying, legendary bluesman? I pondered what sort of medicine the old fellow might need. Hopefully it would be something dramatic, such as nitroglycerin tablets.

"We gotta drive somewhere," Cotton said.

He was whispering and so I whispered back, "Okay, let me get my friend. He has the car."

"Hurry now," Cotton said.

It did not occur to me to question why Cotton had entrusted this medical task to me, rather than (say) his manager, or a person in some way affiliated with his tour. I was really a very sheltered human being.

Nonetheless, I fetched Holden and Cotton stood up and placed himself in our custody.

"You all got a liquor store around here?" he said.

"I guess," Holden said. "We can find one."

The situation now dawned on me: my dying bluesman was in fact an alcoholic, dying, perhaps, of alcoholism. This put a certain spin on the current scenario, made it seem potentially less heartwarming and more sort of criminally negligent. At the same time, I felt I'd committed myself to the cause of James Cotton. He was the star and therefore in charge of the unfolding events and I was, in this respect, merely following orders.

And so we three proceeded toward a rear exit door, Cotton tottering along happily, until we heard someone address him from the other side of the stage. A brief low-speed chase ensued. The manager—not wanting to attract undue attention—walked briskly after us. Cotton reached for the door. "Hurry now," he muttered gamely. His manager drew closer, softly calling, "James? James? Where do you think you're *going*, James?"

I was not granted further interview time.

3. *Regaling Dan Bern During His Pre-show Bowel Movement* Let me start by noting that my admiration for Bern dated back to an advance copy of his 1996 EP, *Dog Boy Van*, and quickly blossomed into full-scale dementia. Bern is best known these days as the guy who wrote the songs for the faux biopic *Walk Hard: The Dewey Cox Story*. But back in the late nineties, there was a small but stubborn contingent of us who considered him the heir apparent to Dylan: an adenoidal midwestern Jew who wrote brilliant rambling folk songs. "The day that Elvis died it was like a mercy killing," he sang, and my chest went pitter-patter.

I'd been waiting years to see Bern in concert when he finally played a show in Cambridge. I showed up hours early and milled around the merch table. I bought his mimeographed book of poetry. I waited. He eventually appeared and was set upon by a pack of smitten college kids.

"What is there to do around here?" Bern said. Someone mentioned candlepin bowling. He looked at the prettiest of the girls—she had short black hair and a generous bosom—and said, "What are *you* going to do?" The girl blushed. They agreed to meet up later. I was mildly disgusted and deeply impressed. Then Bern excused himself and went into the bathroom.

Why did I follow him into that bathroom? I suppose because I do not have a generous bosom and therefore assumed my only possible audience with Bern would be an at-sink rendezvous during which I could ask him to sign his book. This would segue to a broader discussion of literature and art, one so enthralling that Bern would insist we hang after the show, to hell with getting blown by the black-haired chick on lane twelve!

He was in the stall. I had a brief Larry Craigish notion: I could sit down in the stall next to him. But it was one of those giant handicapped jobbers and I couldn't quite get myself there. I considered exiting the bathroom, but that struck me as a form of surrender. I was a fan, after all. I had pimped the man's work far and wide. Without dudes like me, there were no easy blowjobs. If you really thought about it (and I was really thinking about it, there in the bathroom, as only a DF can), the guy owed me. Bern had been in the stall for a minute or two by now. So I said, in a loud nervous voice, the kind of voice you might use upon greeting someone at a crowded party, "Hey, Dan Bern!"

There was a long silence.

I guess it sort of goes without saying that I was not seeing things from Bern's point of view.

"Yeah?" he said finally.

"I just wanted to say, you know, I love your music!"

More silence.

"I'm a big fan," I added.

Bern said, at most, if I didn't just make this up, "Thanks."

"Yeah, I've got all your records, all the way back to *Dog Boy Van*. I reviewed a couple of them for the *Miami New Times*, the weekly down in Miami, I was the music editor down there for a while, though I'm a writer now, you know, fiction, poetry, that kind of thing, though I still do some editing on the side just to pay the bills, whatever, actually we might know a few people in common . . ." I began listing people we might know in common.

At a certain point, two guys walked into the bathroom. I was talking excitedly in the direction of a bathroom stall. They stared.

"Right!" I said. "Okay. We can talk later on, I guess."

4. Nearly Getting Stomped by Kid Frost   I very much doubt you've heard of Kid Frost, but I spent most of 1990 listening to his debut, *Hispanic Causing Panic*. I was an Anglo carpetbagger living in El Paso and trying to expand my Spanish vocabulary beyond *chimichanga*. Listening to Frost's raspy sermons about street life made me feel as if I were bonding with the city's Chicano underclass. (I was not.)

When Frost's name appeared as an opening act on a rap tour heading to El Paso, I arranged a phone interview. Frost did a lot of cussing. He was in a dark mood, he said, because his cousin had just gotten arrested. It was the sort of detail that made me feel we had bonded.

This, I suspect, is why I felt no compunction about approaching him when I spotted him swaggering through the lobby of the arena before his set. "Kid Frost," I called out. "Mr. Frost, or maybe it's just Frost! I'm from the *El Paso Times*. I interviewed you for the newspaper!"

Frost glared at me with his hooded eyes. He was radiating menace, as befitted a budding hip-hop star in a public setting. But my Drooling Fanaticism wouldn't allow me to see this. I assumed Kid Frost had read my glowing profile and felt embarrassed. Kid Frost was *shy*.

"I'm a big fan of your music," I said. "*Fanático grande.*"

Kid Frost continued to glare at me (shyly!). Because I could think of nothing else to say and because I imagined referencing his cousin would somehow make me sound "down" with his "struggle" and that of La Raza in general, I added, "I hope your cousin is doing okay."

His eyes narrowed. "What'd you hear about my cousin?" he said.

"Nothing," I said. "Just that he was, you know—"

"Don't fucking say *nothing* about my cousin."

Frost scanned the lobby for potential witnesses.

"Sorry," I said. "I was just, because remember we talked about—"

Frost flexed the fingers of his right hand and leaned toward me. The air between us was ripe with Paco Rabanne cologne, his, mine, ours. He murmured something in Spanish, of which all I could make out was a conjugation of the verb *chingar*: to fuck. Did Kid Frost want to fuck me?

He set his hand on my chest and gave a brisk shove.

Shit, I thought, *I have somewhat misread this situation and am now going to get boot-stomped by a guy in patent leather shoes.*

But Frost saw something that gave him pause (a security guard, it would turn out) and brushed past me.

5. Smoking More Pot Than Bob Marley and Possibly the Wailers Before Entering Graceland Why did I do this? Because I was secretly dreading Graceland, the preening necrophilia of the scene, that tawdry American knack for spiritual projection, for worshipping the wrong savior for the wrong reason in the wrong way. I figured getting stoned might make the experience seem more profound, and therefore less depressing. It's the same doomed theory I continually apply to Hollywood films.

I needed Graceland to be profound, at least a little, because I had driven seven hundred miles to be there, as a favor to my lovesick friend Tina who was, unbeknownst to me, a Devout Elvis Person. It was a bit like discovering someone is Born Again. You have to respect the purity, but you don't really want to hear the rap. So I smoked bowl after bowl until I could no longer locate my mouth. We boarded a bus full of more Devout Elvis People, southern grandmas with big purses and sullen midwestern Goth kids and packs of cameraed Japanese. As we entered the estate, they fell into a collective and dreadful hush.

A female staffer (blond, hot-kinked, erotically nervous) met us in the foyer with our audio kits. I kept forgetting I was wearing head-phones and yelling at Tina: "HEY! YOU KNOW WHAT THE JUNGLE ROOM LOOKS LIKE? IT'S LIKE AFRICA IF THEY SOLD AFRICA ON THE *HOME SHOPPING NETWORK*! WHY ARE THE WALLS COV-ERED IN TWINE? DID ELVIS' PARENTS REALLY SLEEP IN THESE BEDS? COULDN'T HE HAVE GOTTEN THEM BIGGER BEDS? THAT'S FUCKED UP."

This was Graceland in a nutshell. It was supposed to be about the grandeur of the King, but it kept being about his humiliation: Elvis sprawls on the white couchette in his media room with a plate of bacon, watching three TVs at once. Then he tries to beat back the fat with bennies and he can't sleep at night so he sits up composing his list of enemies. Then he shoots at his radar range. Then he visits Nixon. Then he does karate and pulls something. Then he can't get out of bed and they cancel the tour. Then he falls off his toilet and dies.

Devout Elvis People were everywhere, snapping photos of gold records. The reverence was suffocating. I retreated to the top of a car-peted staircase and found myself staring into a darkened room. Where was I? Where was Tina? Why was there a rope across the doorway with a sign reading NO TRESPASSING? Wasn't trespassing more or less the business model at Graceland?

A voice beckoned me from the bottom of the stairs. "Sir!" A young man stood frowning at me. The name tag on his oversized blazer read KEVIN.

"Where am I?" I said.

"Those are private quarters, sir."

"People still live here?"

Kevin said, "You need to come downstairs, sir. Right now."

Kevin was right. I needed to come downstairs. I needed to flee Graceland and take a hot shower. But the pot wouldn't let me. It kept telling me that I should leap over the rope and breach the private quarters and find the bathroom where Elvis breathed his last and drop a symbolic deuce. Bad pot. *Bad.*

"Are we going to have a problem?" Kevin said. He was trying to sound official. He touched at the tender spray of acne on his right cheek.

I found Tina outside and we proceeded from the shooting range to the nearby Meditation Garden. Elvis was actually buried in the Meditation Garden, which I did not understand at all. Did Elvis consider death a form of extreme meditation? I wanted to ask Tina, but she was weeping. Nearly everyone around me was weeping. They were weeping and taking photos of each other and I knew that, in a few weeks, when they got their photos from Graceland back, they'd gaze at these images of themselves weeping in front of Elvis's grave and start weeping again. And this thought made me sad for America, the great disconnect between our personal causes for grief and our actual tears, and though I was not sad enough to start weeping myself I did flee to the gift shop where, in a final spasm of defiance, I shoplifted an official Elvis wristwatch.

5a. Failing to Recognize (the Very Next Morning) That the Man Preaching at Al Green's Full Gospel Tabernacle Church Was, in Fact, the Reverend Al Green, Even After He Began Singing "Let's Stay Together" Because I'd Assumed Al Green Was Fat Like Barry White No, I was not stoned.

7

On the Varieties of Fanatical Experience

I've been trying to make the case—in my own discombobulated case-making fashion—for Drooling Fanaticism as a spiritual condition, that music is, for some of us, the chosen path toward what William James called "a larger, richer, more satisfying life." James was talking about God, but I'll happily regard that as a term of convenience for That Which We Worship with Irrational and Perhaps Head-Banging Glee.

In fact, I'm willing to argue at this point that we are all Drooling Fanatics, that every single human being carries within him or her the need for music and that we differ only in matters of degree and expression. If this were another sort of book—a book with intellectual self-respect, for instance—I would support this assertion with a tantalizing anthropological survey of musical devotion within indigenous cultures, and assorted neurological data vector astonishments. Instead, we'll all have to settle for another bleak memory from my days as a bumbling lothario. This one takes place in various provinces of Eastern Europe, where I traveled in the spring of 1997 to woo a beautiful exchange student and was mistakenly bludgeoned by the Rosetta Stone of pop music.

No matter where I went for those two weeks one song greeted me, from the Charles Bridge to the Warsaw Ghetto, from the flashing discos of Bohemia to the house parties of Katowice, from the street corners of Prague to the decrepit jazz clubs of East Berlin. Everyone was playing "Macarena." Everyone was singing "Macarena." Everyone was dancing the Macarena, a synchronized routine in which:

- The dancer extends his arms forward, palms down, then flips his arms over on the beat.
- The dancer sets his hands on his shoulders, the back of his head, and his hips.
- The dancer executes a pelvic rotation in time with the line "Ehhh, Macarena!" simultaneously executing a 90-degree jump-and-turn maneuver so as to repeat the same routine all over again.
- Steve shoots himself in the skull.

But okay, here's the point, which is not to belittle the "Macarena" for its clobbering monotony, its almost heartrending dearth of imagination, but on the contrary to hail its popularity. What more powerful testament can there be to the universal psychotropic power of music? I myself despise "Macarena," and yet I have been humming it for the past three days and my two-year-old daughter is now humming it and I'm pretty sure *she will never stop.*

A second major point is that Drooling Fanatics, while sharing certain essential sensitivities, express these sensitivities in distinct manners. We should not be lumped into a single vast Fanatic ghetto. On the contrary, we should be lumped into various smaller ghettos. A brief survey of the afflicted now ensues:

The Music Douche

To properly capture the essence of Douchedom will require a return to the era of the "record store," in my case a dusty emporium known as Disc Diggers, located in Somerville's Davis Square, where, despite being a regular for ten years, despite subsidizing what was clearly a failing enterprise, I was invariably abused. Typically, I would find a CD that looked interesting and ask a clerk if I could listen to it on the portable player I brought for just such a purpose. This would be the clerk who looked like Ric Ocasek and not the clerk who looked like Bunny Wailer though they were both perpetually surly, as was every other single employee in that store with the exception of the young hot girl whom rest of the clerks despised with the exception of the Bunny Wailer dude who was (I'm pretty sure) shtuping her. Ric would say no. It was the singular pleasure of his life to say no to guys like me.

Record stores have always been ground zero for Music Douche-dom. What made Disc Diggers unique was the variety on display. Bunny Wailer was the Reggae Douche. Ric Ocasek was the Metal Douche. There was also an Alt-Country Douche, an emaciated Punk Douche, a trucker cap–festooned Low-Fi Douche, a bearded and gnomic Jazz Douche. For a few months in the late nineties, they even hired a Grunge Douche. What united all these guys was an aura of self-conscious failure. A number had failed as musicians. Some had failed in less specific ways, as disc jockeys or producers or even (God help us) music critics. And thus they'd landed in a used CD shop, where they wed the inexhaustible resentment of retail wage slavery to the calm sadism of minor bureaucrats. I was endlessly vulnerable to their contempt. I secretly hoped my purchases would meet their approval. They never did.

The question naturally arises: But aren't you a Douche, Steve? You sure seem like a douche.

Not really.

In fact, I'm closer these days to a *Music Geek* (subcategory: *Aging*), which is in its crucial aspect the opposite of a Douche. Geeks may indulge in situational snobbery, but their general outlook is absent of malice. The more virulent form, *Inveterate Hipsterism*, often exudes a Douchy imperiousness. But Hipsters dream of conversion. The true Douche dreams only of crucifixion.

Concert Queens

My hairstylist Linda is the foremost example here. The first hint is her cutting station, which is decorated with photos of Billy Corgan, who glares at you, bald and transcendently sullen, as if your decision to bother with hair—the styling of it, the having of it—is an offense. The other indicator is that no matter when I come in for a haircut Linda has always just seen a show. She has always just seen a triple bill of Poison, Quiet Riot, and Queensrÿche. She has always just seen Steely Dan and Elton John and Public Enemy. ("I was in the front row. Flavor Flav threw a beer right at my head!") She has always just seen Black Sabbath, and has detailed opinions about the relative merit of the band's new lead singer.

I once asked Linda, who is well into her thirties now, how many concerts she'd seen in her life. Her final estimate was 3500. She has employed the Bedazzler[10] on hundreds of occasions. She has been trampled. She once wound up on Weird Al Yankovic's tour bus—"his driver is into gay porn, in case you're wondering"—while her friend enjoyed the dubious carnal pleasures of Weird Al. And she herself once followed Whitesnake back to their hotel. She was seventeen at the time.

It's important to make a distinction between Concert Queens and groupies, though. Groupies attach themselves to particular bands and the attraction is centrally erotic. They dream of sexual possession.

---

10. Noun, *buh-**daz**-ler*: 1. A plastic device used to apply rhinestones, studs, or other shiny objects to clothing. 2. The quintessence of American imperial achievement.

Concert Queens might find Ozzy Osbourne sexy, but they don't really want to peel off his soggy underwear. They hunger for the bustle and the clamor and the adrenaline—the transporting pageantry of the show.

The last time I visited Linda, she had just come off three consecutive Pat Benatar concerts.

"What's it like seeing Pat Benatar three times in a row?" I asked.

"It's the exact same show every night," Linda said, *"note for note."*

Her tone suggested she recognized how depressing this fact was. But Linda is devout. She happily suspends all critical faculties when the stage lights come up. "It doesn't really matter who's playing" was how she put it. "The music just takes me away."

I wasn't sure how I felt about this. It's Linda and her ilk, after all, who keep the Benatars of the world on life support, who reduce rock and roll from a subversive cultural force to a tranquilizing commodity. And then on the other hand . . . who the hell am I to question the needs of my fellow Fanatics? There is, after all, such a giddy quality to the way Linda recounts shows. And she isn't a giddy person by nature. During the time I've known her, Linda has dealt with some crushing losses. She's watched the love of her life slip away from her, into a life of illness and addiction.

This is why she needs the shows. They aren't merely a form of nostalgic meditation, but a means of feeling alive in the face of misfortune. Some people turn to prayer or self-help affirmations or marathon running. Linda has concerts. "You know what I really love?" she told me one time. "When you get home from a show and you put your head down on the pillow and all you can hear is ringing. Because that means it was really loud and I was really close. I was right up against the speakers."

Collectors

If you're wondering if you're a collector, ask yourself two questions.

1. Do I own too many records?

2. Do my friends and family feel I own too many records?

If your respective answers are No and Yes, you're a Collector.

Consider Angela Sawyer. The first thing she told me when I visited her was, "I don't think of myself as someone who has an overly large collection." The second thing she told me was, "Watch your step." We were sitting in Angela's bedroom, which is perhaps 120 square feet. It contained ten thousand records. The living room contained another five thousand records, semiofficial property of Weirdo Records, the shop she runs out of her Somerville apartment.

Most of the records in Angela's personal collection fall into what she calls the "extreme" category: outsider noise rock, field recordings of frogs, sing-alongs featuring guys in cardigans strumming banjos. Angela does not like these albums ironically. She is truly enraptured by tracks such as "Pammie's on a Bummer"—Sonny Bono's account of a girl who smokes pot for the first time and turns into a prostitute. This is what sets Collectors apart from garden variety Drooling Fanatics. They've listened to all their albums and studied their historical context and formed thoughtful, even tortured, opinions about them. They're obsessed with aesthetics.

This offers a stark contrast to, for instance, *Music Snobs*, who are obsessed with constructing an identity based on the contents of their iPod. Snobs want to know whether a record is "good" or "bad" and (most important) what these judgments say about them within a given social milieu. Collectors have pretty much given up relating to anyone else who isn't a Collector.

But the question remains: what turns a Drooling Fanatic into a

Collector? My wife would certainly like to know. She believes I have a retentive neurosis, a notion I don't dispute. It's no coincidence that, in the years I was amassing my collection, I lived in no fewer than eight cities. My discs and tapes were the only objects that came with me. The rest of the memorabilia—the posters and photos and letters that felt so essential at the time—got ditched in closets.

Still, I would argue that most Collectors are not guilty of an acquisitive defect but a peculiar blend of sloth and reverence. We're too lazy to sort through our records *and* philosophically averse to disposing of them. I have certainly tried to purge. Every few months I head downstairs to our Serial Killer Room, fully intending to *do something*. Here's what happens. I drag out one of my eleven milk crates full of CDs and I start sorting through them and inevitably find an album I haven't heard in years, the unsung soul-pop masterpiece *Back in the 90's* by the band Hobex, say, and the moment I put it on I'm transported back to Greensboro and the sweet misery of that era. It all returns: the fuming solitude, the sexy poet who lanced my heart, the yeasty clouds billowing forth from the extravagantly misnamed New York Pizza. And I think: Throw this album out? Is my wife crazy? It's a fucking time machine!

This is the thing misunderstood by those who don't have unreasonable music collections. The record is not simply a storage device. Its value resides in the particular set of memories and emotional associations held by its owner. These are inseparable from the physical object, which is no longer a physical object but an article of faith.

Semi-Pros

Most musicians self-identify as Drooling Fanatics, and they exhibit many of the prescribed behaviors. But they don't count in my book, because they violate the main prerequisite which is that you're *not a musician.*

There is, however, an entire population who has twined their lives around music, somewhat less than profitably. I'm thinking about the grizzled buskers and part-time cellists and YouTube aspirants, the folks who occupy that eager nexus between amateur and professional. Most of all I'm thinking about my pal Clay Martin.

I met Clay in the summer of 1988. We were glorified interns working at newspapers in Phoenix, appropriately stunned by the climatic artifice of the city. It was Death Valley with condos, a genuine Marxist nightmare. Our commute was like sitting in a Holly Hobbie Oven.

I was in the nascent stages of my Fanaticism, having just earned my college degree, and I squandered much of that summer bickering with my roommate over the moral intent of the Warren Zevon song "Boom Boom Mancini" and attempting to find a woman stupid enough to fuck me.

I wanted to be rooming with Clay. He was handsome and sweet-natured and he played guitar. Occasionally, he and his roommate Gerry let me sit in when they jammed. This meant Clay on lead and Gerry playing, if I remember this right, bongos, while I attempted to find the single note on a harmonica that didn't destroy whatever feeble melodic momentum we'd wandered into. As happens when you're twenty-one years old, a single pleasing string of notes, combined with alcohol and sleep deprivation, led us to the conclusion that we should start a band, or that we already perhaps had started a band and simply needed a name for licensing and touring purposes. We settled on "Coy and Smiley." The band lasted a grand total of twenty-seven minutes. Then Gerry fell asleep.

At the end of the summer, Clay headed up to Redmond, Washington, where he found a job with a new company called Microsoft. We all felt sorry for Clay. Poor Clay. He was never going to be a real journalist. He was going to become a Sad Computer Guy Loser who sent us postcards with cats wearing human clothing.

Some years later, I visited Seattle and caught up with Clay. He'd taken an early retirement from Microsoft. He had a gorgeous girl-friend and a home in the coolest neighborhood on earth. He had launched his own record label. Oh, and he'd also formed his own band, which was heading to Europe for a tour. This was one of those mid-thirties moments when you take a look at the stale, half-chewed bagel your life has become and kiss jealousy on its smoky mouth.

A year later, Clay came east for a tour with his band, Sushirobo. I secretly hoped Sushirobo might suck, but I was out of luck. They sounded like Devo soaked in absinthe, frantic and playful and weird, with skronks of guitar noise and swirling distortion. Clay played bass. The instrument seemed to deliver small hammering shocks to his body. It was a thrilling set, though I seemed to be the only person in the bar listening. The rest of the patrons (young women mostly, in the black makeup of neglect) were there to see the next act, a metal band from Worcester.

Afterward, I ran up to congratulate Clay and his mates. I assumed they would be whisked off to a hotel in a limo by their label. Then I remembered Clay *was* the label. They wound up crashing at my place. It was quickly made apparent how grueling it was to tour as an obscure art rock band, to drive hundreds of miles at close quarters, to absorb the fair complaints of wives and bosses back home, to walk around in clothing stiff with sweat, to dump your laundry into the washing machines of kind strangers, to maintain self-belief in the face of such persistent disregard. I'd gotten it all wrong, as usual.

Sushirobo, for all its brilliance, would be gone before long. Anyone could see that. So would most of the other bands on his label. This was what made Clay a courageous figure. He was a Semi-Pro, like most musicians on this earth, a guy driven to reckless action by his Drooling Fanaticism. Music had deranged him in precisely the man-ner required to locate his heroism.

Rock's Top Ten Religious Freaks

1. Bob Dylan

Nobody confounded the messianic aspects of his stardom better than Zimmy. He went straight from the coked-up carnival of the Rolling Thunder Revue to Bible school. F'ing brilliant.

2. Johnny Cash

Endorsed cold-blooded murder ("I shot a man in Reno, just to watch him die . . .") in front of a prison crowd consisting of cold-blooded murderers. Later kicked by an ostrich, resulting in abdominal injury, resulting in painkiller addiction, resulting in rehab and rebirth. God I love country music.

3. Prince

The second most famous Jehovah's Witness to sing about masturbation. (*Beat It!*)

4. Cat Stevens aka Yusuf Islam

Converted to Islam at the height of his stardom, sold his guitars for charity, and devoted himself to religious philanthropy. World's first career-suicide bomber?

5. Dave Mustaine

Metallica reject and Megadeth leader refused to play a gig with the band Rotting Christ. "I would prefer not to play on concerts with satanic bands," he told fans. "That doesn't mean I won't."

6. Donna Summer

Her orgasmic moaning fueled a twenty-minute version of "Love to Love You Baby," which she dedicated to Christ.

7. Alice Cooper

Stage show featured gothic torture and mock executions via electric chair and guillotine. Like a passion play, but with strobe lights.

8. Little Richard

The man who inspired Dylan! Added bonus: totally not one bit gay.

9. Gordon Gano

Violent Femmes front man sacrificed his devout Baptist-cred when he sold "Blister in the Sun" to Wendy's, leading to the ill-fated ad campaign: *Wendy's burgers—so delish they blister in the sun!*

10. Michael Henry McBrain

Iron Maiden drummer dressed up as the devil on the "Number of the Beast" world tour in 1982. Then accepted Jesus Christ as his personal savior 666 times.

How Hip-Hop Sounds in a Canyon

The Drooling Fanatic seeks a sense of mastery before committing serious listening time to a musical style. He or she needs to understand what the genre is about, what makes it tick.

Back in 1983, for instance, I saw my first punk rock show. This was during my ill-fated Week as a Punk Rocker, which coincided with my ill-fated Attempt to Sleep with a Punk Rock Chick. The venue was an all-ages club next to the Palo Alto Co-op—nothing says punk rock like bulk bin granola—and the band in question, just formed, was called the Red Hot Chili Peppers. I found the performance confusing. The songs didn't really start or end, they just kind of crashed into being. The scrawny guys in front reacted by smashing into each other so as to draw blood in some charismatic fashion. For their encore, the Peppers came out wearing nothing but tube socks over their genitals. "That's a band going *nowhere*," I announced. And yet the Peppers' appeal was clear: they allowed disaffected suburban kids to deliver a loud *fuck off* to the spangled costumes of New Wave.

I'd never really gotten what hip-hop was about, either, until the Wednesday afternoon in 1995 when Frankie Tomasino proposed we bail on work and catch an afternoon ballgame. We tore up I-95. Frankie had his thighs jammed under the wheel of his red Civic and a beer propped in his crotch. As we sped north, the radio's static resolved into a happy liquid throbbing. This was The Bomb, Miami's premier pirate station, which broadcast from a bunker within the vast rutted perimeter of Liberty City. The Bomb didn't operate like commercial stations. The songs never really stopped and the DJ talked over all of them. He took phone calls from female listeners and hung up on those who refused to reciprocate his intimacies. "That's not riding," he told them. "Let's ride." There were really only two categories in his world. Either you could ride or you couldn't ride.

Frankie hardly ever got to listen to The Bomb because his job was to sell advertising, which required merchants with an ad budget, of which Liberty City had few, the retail sector running more toward junkyards and unlicensed drink houses. The music swirled around us. I tried to pin down the melody—was it Billy Preston? Bill Withers?—but the song kept expanding to incorporate new samples, squiggles of trumpet, barrelhouse piano, bone-crushing drum loops. "What *is* this?" I said. Frankie grinned. He looked like a drowsy wolf.

A Buick pulled alongside us. The driver was a big black guy in a tasseled nylon bandana. He glanced over at Frankie and Frankie glanced over at him and they both punched the gas. The pavement hummed beneath us. Palm trees ripped past. We were screaming down a highway littered with chunks of Jersey barrier, surrounded by immigrants and geezers, drivers unhinged from the laws of vehicular common sense. Normally, I would have sailed straight into a conniption. But the music was doing funny things to my fear receptors, blotting out the lethal possibilities. All I could think was: *Wow, this is the coolest thing that's ever happened to me.*

I was not unfamiliar with hip-hop, of course. I had pledged allegiance to Run-D.M.C. and Kid Frost. But the stuff pumping out of Frankie's speakers was of a different order. It was the sort of music I always suspect the black community keeps hidden from the rest of us, the hydroponic shit grown in underground labs and silenced whenever Whitey comes within earshot.

Some ancient, unfortunate breed of Ford materialized in front of us and Frankie flicked into the next lane. I glanced up and took note of the horizon, which was jittering, and here I began murmuring things. *Hey man,* I murmured, *maybe we should lay off. Your car's kind of shaking. There's cops around here. Seriously.* Frankie turned the radio up; the music was more or less driving the car at this point.

We pulled even with the Buick. We were at a hundred, then 105, and the car truly was shaking and I began to think, regrettably, about Arthur McDuffie, the black motorcyclist who, on this very highway, in 1979, engaged police in a high-speed chase that ended with a bunch of white cops cracking his skull like an egg, triggering one of the worst race riots in American history, a scenario toward which we seemed to be hurtling, my proposed headline reading:

DRAG RACING JEW TRIGGERS INNER CITY KILLFEST
Dazed Suspect Tells Investigators "They Can't Ride"

Then the Buick's motor started to spew smoke and his back end fishtailed and Frank chose this moment to hoist the beer from his crotch and toast the guy in the Buick, who was also listening to The Bomb. This was a large, angry human being, someone who, it seemed reasonable to suppose, was not in the habit of being emasculated by a Cuban guy in business casual. Any second, I expected him to pull a weapon from beneath his seat, or perhaps his lap, and shoot my face off. Instead, he eased off the gas and waved his middle finger. Frankie howled. He pounded the top of the steering wheel. The music thumped on and on. "That's how you ride," the DJ shouted. His point being: *This* was hip-hop, the extraction of joy from mayhem.

The Canyon

Did I become one of those annoying overnight hip-hop fans? Not exactly. But I did listen to a great deal of the stuff that year, because I spent much of it in the James Scott Homes, the largest housing development in Liberty City, which was, like every other low-income housing project in this country, a village of women and children, a vast colony of dependence where wishes perished in unromantic stillness. Residents had a special nickname for Scott. They called it the Canyon.

I had come to the Canyon to report on a disputed tenant board election, and decided there was a bigger story to be told, about what it was like for the kids growing up there. The idea was to get beyond the usual drive-by bullshit. For the most part I just hung out. I played spades with the mamas and brought the kids giant waxed boxes of Church's Chicken and listened to the clamor of TV jingles and sirens and video game gunfire.

The local playlist consisted of singles by artists such as "Big Mike" and "27th Ave" and "that fat boy Andre that steps with that girl that got a baby by Sherman" whose battered demos, cassettes mostly, scrawled with contact info, were passed from hand to hand. The songs were superb: extremely violent, extremely witty, an antidote to life as it actually existed in the Canyon, where the boys dealt drugs to transform themselves into figures of consequence and the girls had babies for the same reason, where the sheer tedium made people itchy for tragedy.

I'm thinking now of the night I arrived in the Canyon to find that a boy named Trey had been shot in the face. Trey himself was eventually presented to me. His face had been shot, no question about it. There was some discussion as to whether I might want to see the entry and exit wounds. I said no, it was probably best to leave the bandages be.

This shooting was a sad piece of news, and there were obligatory expressions of distress by the prevailing mamas. But the general vibe was one of breathless excitement. A story could now be told and retold. A cause for revenge had been inked. The morose and mangled Trey, a marginal figure before this trouble, was now a celebrity.

Dear Mama

This was the summer of 2Pac's "Dear Mama," which played in heavy rotation at the Canyon's holiday barbecues and birthday parties and wakes. It was a love letter from all the wayward boys lost to the streets or the great time capsule of incarceration, a hymn to maternal endurance set to a luscious Spinners riff. "Even as a crack fiend, mama/You always was a black queen, mama," 2Pac sang.

Which was a lovely sentiment, full of Christian mercy, but also completely mystifying to me because wouldn't being a crack fiend put a crimp in your mothering capacities, in terms of, for instance, spending your money on crack as opposed to food? You will forgive my naïveté. I was a Drooling Fanatic, not a social anthropologist.

Still, it didn't take a genius to see that most of the mamas (and aunties and grannies) in the Canyon were falling down on the job. I watched a lot of kids get smacked and marveled at the variety of objects with which one could smack a child: a shoe, a school binder, a block of cheese. One particularly remorseless creature, Doris, attempted to have her son labeled learning disabled, because such a label would trigger an extra social security payment. And Tammy— I didn't even realize she *had* kids until the three of them escaped from the upstairs bedroom where she had them locked up.

It was the boys with whom I came to spend most of my time. They were desperate for any kind of adult male attention and settled for me because, well, I was available. These were the boys who listened to hip-hop most devoutly, who blasted their eardrums with the songs.

They knew all the words to "Gangsta's Paradise" and "Ready to Die" and "Shook Ones, Part 2."

When I pondered it—and I did a lot, as I sped away from the Canyon, down the barren streets of Liberty City, with its bales of razor wire, its battered churches and liquor stores, toward my suddenly luxurious-seeming studio in Miami Beach—these songs were all asking the same question: *How did one fashion a life of consequence from one without prospects?* It was an American question, a question about opportunity, and it hung over the Canyon like a dark fog.

Ghostland

Sometimes I brought the boys with me. Sure. I had a car. I struck everybody involved as a responsible adult. Why not take a few of the shavers to the library or the mall or the beach? That was what they wanted, more than a big brother, more than a mentor: a getaway driver. It got to the point where there'd be a line of them waiting, kids I'd never seen before, whose mothers or aunties or legal guardians I didn't even know.

It was on one of these excursions that a kid named Nookie slipped a tape into my cassette deck. I just about drove off the road. The melodies were dark and percolating, a marriage of vintage jazz samples and loping beats. The lyrics were poetic without sentiment. "Who is this?" I said.

"Simeon and them other niggers," Nookie said.

"Wait a second," I said. "You *know* these guys?"

Nookie's face assumed an expression of indulgence. He set about explaining the connection, which involved a cousin who designed the logo for Simeon and his crew, Lastrawze they were called. According to Nookie, they operated out of an apartment on West Dixie north of Cagni Park.

Then a song came on that was unlike anything I'd ever heard, a swirl of sirens and trumpets and a single moaning note wrung from the neck of a guitar. "Where I'm At (Ghostland)" was a travelogue of the grim precincts where the Strawze had grown up. But it was really about the emotional state boys were forced to occupy in such places, which lay somewhere between sorrow and nihilism, which was exhausting because it required a constant expenditure of courage, which treated the smallest sign of vulnerability as an invitation to assault, and made it impossible for them, ever, to simply relax. There are some guys, Simeon explained "who run around and crack jokes/And now some nigs is in the cemetery doing backstrokes."

This was all the more striking because the "Miami sound" of that era was dominated by 2 Live Crew, and expressly designed to inspire the greased vibration of female butt cheeks. Lastrawze cribbed obscure licks from Grover Washington and quoted Shakespeare. They rejected the gold-plated bluster of gangsta rap in favor of an authentic hip-hop naturalism.

And often there'd be some moment during my field trips with those boys when one or another of them was momentarily frightened or humiliated and the trust went flickering out of their eyes. I could see it happen. The part of themselves open to feeling simply vanished. They had slipped silently off to Ghostland.

Everything's (Not Really) Gonna Be All Right

One Saturday, I drove them to the zoo. The trip started full of hope but quickly went south because, as much as the boys hated the Canyon and dreaded the prospect of returning there, it was what they knew and where they felt comfortable. They were immigrants in the larger world, uncertain and fragile. It was Boo-Man who melted down at the zoo, no doubt because the zoo was on the same road that led to the correctional facility where his father was doing time. He threw himself against the fence of the peacock enclosure with an abrupt and very real violence, startling the animals, and I bent down to comfort him, but he wouldn't speak or meet my eyes and I could see he was gone to Ghostland.

So we headed home. Just north of the city my Tercel started to heave. I glanced down at the gas gauge, which read *D* for *Dumbshit*. I managed to coast halfway onto a shoulder. Trucks whizzed past us, blaring their horns. The car shook. Then an afternoon storm rolled in and brought with it a downpour straight out of central casting. At this point, the kids had the good sense to panic. I shouted at them to calm-down-calm-down-calm-the-fuck-down-and-stay-in-the-car and ran howling into this biblical deluge. I was going to find gas. That was my bright idea. I had no idea where we were. I couldn't even *see* a sidewalk.

I fell down an embankment. I staggered some miles to a gas station. I paid two guys forty bucks to drive me back to my car. I failed to locate my car. I begged the guys not to abandon me. I considered what would happen if a police officer located my car before I could, what the state statutes might have to say about the reckless endangerment of five minors. Or would this be kidnapping?

It cost me another forty bucks but I did find the car. The kids cheered and talked all at once about who had cried and who hadn't and we went to Little Caesars for a pizza party, during which it began to dawn on me how out of my depth I was. What was I up to, exactly? I wasn't going to adopt any of these kids, or get them a scholarship. I was writing a story about them. I was designing a brochure of their hardships.

And it occurred to me then that hip-hop itself was a brochure, an invitation to consume the destructive grief of the urban underclass. Wasn't that what made the genre so seductive—like the blues, like Negro spirituals—that its vitality arose from the cauldron of racial hardship? Was I supposed to ride with that? But then on the other hand was it right to impose a moral litmus test on music? That seemed repugnant and silly. I was (let's remember) a Drooling Fanatic in my formative days. These sorts of quandaries made me ache with self-importance.

In the end, I finished up my story and got the fuck out of the ghetto and stayed the fuck out of the ghetto (to quote Naughty by Nature) and shut up about my hip-hop fetish, much to the relief of all involved, though I did eventually convince my editors to let me write a story about Lastrawze, a miserably earnest profile I assumed would vault them to stardom. A few weeks later, Nookie informed me that one of the Strawze had gone upstate on gun charges. They were never heard from again.

Interlude:
Winter in America with Gil Scott-Heron

This is as good a time as any to acknowledge Gil Scott-Heron, the great unsung prophet of American music who is often and stupidly hailed as the "Godfather of hip-hop." He is, if anything, its inventor. In 1971, Gil released "The Revolution Will Not Be Televised," the first song to fuse the tradition of the street preacher with that of the soul singer. "Rapper's Delight" by the Sugar Hill Gang would not be released for another decade.

I saw Gil in concert only once, flying from Miami to Washington, D.C., for the chance. I remember almost nothing of that trip aside from the fight I got into with my soon to be ex-girlfriend. It was the sort of fight you relish in the late stages of a long relationship, when you're both hunting for an excuse to hate each other's guts. She took me to this Dominican restaurant that made the best chicken on earth—it certainly smelled that way—and we got up to the counter and she ordered a whole chicken without even consulting me. Wait a second, I said, do you like dark meat or white meat? What does it matter? she said. And I said, It matters because I like dark meat, so if you like dark meat too then we should order by the piece and she sighed the Monumental Sigh of Womankind and said, Fine, I'll eat the white meat! and placed the order and both of us stared at the chickens twirling helplessly on their spits. And of course when we got home she reached for a piece of dark meat and of course I said, See, I knew this would happen and she said, What? then shook her head and we proceeded to the feature attraction, starring the Woman Who Refuses to Think About Anyone Else and the Man So Petty It Boggles the Mind, which lasted for the next thirty-six hours, until I was scheduled to depart, without a farewell, and sort of intentionally peed on her toilet seat.

Why is this my dominant memory of that visit? Why does my mind so dependably seize on the awful? This was a weekend I'd been looking forward to for months, because I'd revered Gil Scott-Heron since my uncle Pete gave me *The Best of Gil Scott-Heron* as a high school graduation gift, back in 1984.

I had no idea what to make of the record at first. It did not sound like "Cruel Summer" by Bananarama. Nor did it sound like "Shark Attack" by Split Enz. The arrangements baffled me. Was this Latin music? Funk? And what of the strange instruments (flute? timbale?). Gil sang beautifully—when he chose to sing. But more often he delivered the words in a sly chant that confused and enthralled me. It's the reason we become enamored of certain singers, I think, because they project the voice we wish to summon within ourselves. His was a masterpiece: deep, resonant, slightly muddied by the South, learned but playful. It was like listening to Richard Pryor and Malcolm X and Barry White in three-part harmony. "The idea concerns the fact that this country wants nostalgia," he explained, in the track "B-Movie."

They want to go back as far as they can even if it's only as far as last week. Not to face now or tomorrow, but to face backwards. And yesterday was the day of our cinema heroes riding to the rescue at the last possible moment. . . . Someone always came to save America at the last moment, especially in B movies. And when America found itself having a hard time facing the future they looked for people like John Wayne. But since John Wayne was no longer available, they settled for Ronald Reagan. And it has placed us in a situation that we can only look at like a B movie.

I'd never heard anyone explain, in language so simple and persuasive, the phony messianism of the Reagan Revolution.

Gil was so prescient as a social critic that people didn't understand what he was talking about half the time. "The Revolution Will Not Be Televised" was (and is) happily misunderstood as a call to arms. In fact, it was a jeremiad about the narcotic effects of screen addiction, how Americans had been lulled into a moral fugue by their televisions. The song was composed in 1970.

More than any single issue, Gil's essential topic was America, how the nation had fallen away from its moral precepts and into ruin, a condition of spiritual malaise that would eventually deliver us the bigotry and psychotic greed of the Bush Era.

If this makes Gil Scott-Heron sound didactic, the fault is mine, for it is the unique talent of the prophet to convert rage into poetry. Gil did so by creating a musical lexicon that ranged from Marvin Gaye to John Coltrane, from James Brown to Tito Puente. "Shut 'Em Down" may have been about nuclear power plants, but it was also a joyous hymn, complete with horn charts and gospel singers. "The Bottle" managed to turn the ravages of addiction into a salsa party.

But I wanted to tell you about the weekend in question, my one and only encounter with Gil. Clearly, it would have been impossible for him to live up to my hopes. Like any good Drooling Fanatic, I expected an ascension. Why not? The club was small and we had good seats.

But Gil.

Gil was a wreck, a muttering wreck, jittery, coked up, or tweaked out on some other cruel amphetamine. He looked skeletal. He couldn't remember the words to his songs and so resorted to vamping. Between songs, he delivered semicoherent soliloquies in which the essential topic was his own desolation.

It was this desolation (I think) that makes me remember the fight about the chicken, which epitomized my own failures, emotional and otherwise, the death of hope being the central drama of that weekend.

I was devastated. I was devastated because I have a birth defect, or possibly some other kind of defect, wherein I expect my musical heroes to shower the air with lilies of patience and wisdom. It didn't occur to me that prophecy—a heightened sensitivity to our moral lapses, a compulsion to declaim—might arise from internal distress. Certainly not in the case of Gil, whose precision as an observer of American folly was the equal of Twain, and who enjoyed the refuge of music.

What I had failed to discern (forgive me, I was still in my twenties) was that true prophets are cursed. They wind up stoned to death. Or alone in the desert, naked and howling. We might take as proof the fact that none of Gil's albums reside in *Rolling Stone*'s Top 500. Such lists are set aside for the true artists of our time, the Def Leppards and TLCs. Gil has become a curious relic, the original uppity rhyming nigger, though he has no more to do with the contemporary hip-hop stars who sample his tracks than Isaiah did with the idolaters of Judah. He preached—with a great and useless eloquence—*against* the delusions of materialism and violence.

Gil himself has become a spectral presence, arrested on drug charges twice in the past few years, imprisoned for ten months on Rikers Island. An old girlfriend of his (or a woman claiming to be) described him as a crack addict living amid squalor. Gil denies this. It's hard to know what to believe. Still, I find myself wanting to defend the guy's honor. The prophet is an idealist unable to silence his disappointment, who lashes out at the world's demons at the risk of awakening his own.

His fate certainly came as no surprise to me. It was clear from the moment I set eyes on him in that club. The years had ravaged his face. His long body flicked like a sparrow's. Time and again he looked in sorrow at a snifter of cognac, which trembled on his keyboard. And when he sang, his voice—once a magnificent gravelly croon—sounded torn.

9

In Which Mr. Joe Henry (Rather Unwittingly) Becomes My Writing Coach

> There was a time when women may have wanted to have my babies. Now it's just middle-aged men who want my guitar pick. Or want to take me home and play me their Joe Henry records.
>
> —Chuck Prophet[11]

In the fall of 1995, I fled the world of journalism for the incredibly lucrative realm of short fiction. This meant driving from Miami to the University of North Carolina at Greensboro, a school I had applied to—and I wish I was kidding here—because of its spiffy four-color brochure. As a parting gift, my friend Jim gave me a homemade tape with a couple of Joe Henry albums. This was the heyday of the No Depression movement and everyone was listening to that one Son Volt record. Jim was a staunch No Depression fan, meaning a) he worshipped country music; and b) he was himself depressed.

I figured Joe Henry was part of that scene. I slipped in the tape, but didn't listen too carefully. Then, up around Pensacola, the song "Short

---

11. Who is Chuck Prophet? Give me another forty pages.

Man's Room" came on. It was an elegant waltz of the sort that might have been played at a barn dance 150 years ago. The narrator seemed like a harmless eccentric at first. Then the fiddle reeled into a minor key and the second verse arrived.

I drink more than maybe I should
But I don't go out when I do
I put my feet up in the window
And I ride my dreams like a canoe

Gradually, it emerged that this guy was the town drunk, a lonely old Indian descending into alcohol dementia. *I once thought I'd live forever,* he explained. *I pitched for the Indian leagues/But now I guess I've learned some better/You're only as good as your knees.*

There were several reasons this song would haunt me throughout grad school. I was an aging jock living in an isolated carriage house with very low ceilings. I was sufficiently addicted to pot that I eventually stalked my dealer. But the main thing was that Joe Henry had written a short story. He had created a character and induced him to tell the truth. I would spend every day of the next two years trying to figure out how the fuck he did it.

I was entering a new phase as a Drooling Fanatic, a kind of literary apprenticeship. There was no TV in my life. E-mail was something you checked once a week at the library. I sat in a sweaty recliner crapping out rough drafts, with the boom box cranked. I read too, of course. I lay on my mattress and frisked library loaners for The Secret of How Not to Suck. But it was the songs that taught me the most.

I read Eudora Welty's "Why I Live at the P.O." like it was the Koran. But it took the Tom Waits ballad "Christmas Card from a Hooker in Minneapolis" for me to grasp the essence of an unreliable narrator, how the poignancy of self-deception resides in its erosion. Cormac McCarthy was a dark monster of language. But if I wanted poetic violence, I turned to Nick Cave's *Murder Ballads*. For reasons that remain unclear, during this time I read *The Executioner's Song*, all 1,072 pages. I couldn't shake the feeling that Steve Earle had covered the same terrain more movingly in the song "Billy Austin." It took him only six minutes.

Time was of the essence—that was the point. Us MFA plebs were like grubby windup dolls. Pull the string and we chanted Chekhov's maxim: cut your first three pages. But Chekhov had nothing on Bruce Springsteen, who opened "Atlantic City" with the greatest first line in the history of pop music: *They blew up the Chicken Man in Philly last night/now they blew up his house too.* Was there a single person on earth who could resist the mystery of this line, with its promise of ruin?

I listened to these songs compulsively, as if by osmosis my writing might improve. It didn't. My characters continued to sit alone in rooms, frittering with artificial woe. They remained dim figures, driven to action not by the defects of their own hearts but by the doomed impulse of all young writers, which is to impress the reader.

What else did I do during those two years? I glommed on to local musicians and hosted hootenannies at my place, during which I stood off to one side curled in a terrified silence. I shaved my head. I threw myself headlong into catastrophic affairs. Songs were the only regular company I kept and the only thing that tempered the self-seriousness with which I was afflicted. To hear the Smoking Popes croon "Let's Hear It for Love" was to realize that erotic turmoil was not a subject suited solely to tragedy, but a variety of cosmic joke.

One of my favorite songs of that era, by a long-forgotten band called the Bogmen, featured a lisping narrator who ricochets between bitter harangues against his ex-girlfriend and tender confessions. The music was geeky R&B of the sort Kool & the Gang would have produced if the Gang had gone to Montessori schools. I must have listened to "Suddenly" a thousand times, and every time I reached the final line (*Suddenly, I have found myself alive*) it roused me. I was trying so hard to absorb this idea: that all our defensive postures boiled down to human longing.

A Brief Disclaimer

Let me assure you that—despite my highfalutin exegeses—I realize how pointless it is to parse song lyrics. Most people simply don't give a shit about the words. I myself spent years not giving a shit about the words. Or worshipping words that were shit. (Sometimes it's hard to tell the difference.) The fact that I can recite Styx's "Renegade" from memory sort of says it all.

I was also an early devotee of R.E.M., whose lyrics were for years famously unintelligible. A few hardcore fans eventually managed to decode Michael Stipe's mumbling, the result being lines such as *There's a splinter in your eye and it reads "react."* Did this discovery dim our devotion? Not one splinter.

This is because our gut response to a song derives from its melody and rhythm. The right tune can revive the baldest clichés and lend dignity to all manner of piffle. It is also why I feel such elaborate gratitude when a musician bothers to treat the language with care. I'm grateful to Bob Dylan for the line *The wind was howling and the snow was outrageous*, with its pained internal rhyme. I'm grateful to Mike Doughty for flicking an ash *like a wild, loose comma* and to John Prine for noticing that *the wind was blowing, especially through her hair* and to Antje Duvekot for her wistful declaration *with all the sand that gets into this world, we should all be motherfucking pearls.*

Because honestly, these folks don't have to bother. Most rockers have made a fine career out of rhyming platitudes. In fact, there's a decent argument to be made that songwriters generally screw themselves when they cavort with literature. Which brings us, unavoidably, to this. . . .

Interlude:
A Mercifully Brief Survey of Prog Rock Lyricism

Progressive rock is what happens when pop stars get a hard-on for high art. It's what happens when they ditch guitar-based blues music in favor of symphonic suites composed on synthesized flute with a 13/7 time signature. More than anything, prog represents the profound danger of literary influence on popular music. Let us examine the case of Jon Anderson, a high school dropout who got his start on washboard in a skiffle band and dreamed of playing professional soccer but who instead joined the band Yes and started wolfing down Eastern philosophies.

"We were in Tokyo on tour," Anderson explains to his fans, "and I had a few minutes to myself in the hotel room before the evening's concert. Leafing through Yogananda's *Autobiography of a Yogi*, I got caught up in a lengthy footnote on page 83. . . . So positive were the Shastras that I could visualize then and there four interlocking pieces of music being structured around them."

I know what you're thinking: who are these Shastras and where can I find their albums? Alas, Anderson is referring to a series of esoteric Buddhist texts. Fortunately, Anderson didn't just read this footnote and forget about it, as so many rock stars might in the addled minutes before a show. No, he used the footnote as the basis for an epic double album entitled *Tales from Topographic Oceans*, which Yes released in 1973.

What is *Tales* about? It is perhaps more efficient to discuss what it is not about. It is not about dropping out of high school. It is not about skiffle. It is not about soccer. It is about, well, here's a tiny taste:

*Craving Penetrations Offer Links with the Self Instructor's Sharp
And Tender Love as We Took to the Air, a Picture of Distance*[12]

I'm not sure it's possible to fathom such profundity, even with a self
instructor's help. But I'll try for a translation: *Help! I am being held pris-
oner by a penetration-craving Yogi! The reason these words seem to be
arranged at random is because I have to speak in code. "Tender love"
means genital fondling. Wait. Shit. He's coming.*

Yes keyboardist Rick Wakeman was so bored by the record that he
once ordered and ate an entire Indian meal on top of his Hammond
organ during a performance. When I heard this story, I thought I might
be in love with Rick Wakeman. Then it came to my attention that Wakeman himself released a solo record called *Journey to the Centre of the
Earth* based on the Jules Verne story and recorded, I'm afraid, with a
full orchestra. My favorite passage is entitled "The Battle." It features
a clash between two giant sea monsters "rising out of the angry sea"
and ends with this pulse-racing play-by-play:

Crocodile teeth, lizard's head, bloodshot eye, stained ocean red

---

12. Oh, how I wish I could quote the rest of this song! But I cannot. I cannot because
to do so would require express written consent from one or more multinational music
corporations—which, it turns out, is only a little more difficult to secure than permission to reprint Blackwater's internal memos—plus an unspecified payment, to be
absorbed by your faithful Fanatic. So: yet another obstacle to writing about music.
Despite the fact that there are literally hundreds of websites archiving song lyrics on
the Internet, and that virtually anyone can quote lyrics, or, hell, even stream music to
their heart's content online, and despite the fact that most lyrics are of nominal literary
value once stripped from their musical context—i.e., Miller, Steve, *I speak of the pompa-
tus of love*—despite all of this, music publishers require, under the so-called Fair Use
doctrine (an Orwellian construction if ever I've heard one) that authors not quote more
than two lines or fifteen words without said consent, lest they be sued to the bejesus by
a goateed lawyer with a vanity plate reading *U R BROKE*. And thus if I seem to be, in
the course of this book, making elaborate and pathetically obvious efforts to limit my
use of lyrics, now you know why. The end.

Journey sold fourteen million copies. Jethro Tull's 1973 concept album *Passion Play* was a number one record in the United States despite—or perhaps because of—lyrics like this:

> *And your little sister's immaculate virginity wings away*
> *on the bony shoulders of a young horse named George*

If you want to understand where the defiant musical ineptitude and proud grunting of punk rock came from, you have only to look back to prog, a genre built on the spectacle of overcompensation. You will find the spirit of prog in the lute compositions of Sting, the agonizing tirades of Trent Reznor, and yes, even in Toto's searing cultural explorations—wherever there are insecure rock stars maxing out the credit card of their own talent.

How Writers Sing

The lesson here is pretty obvious: musicians should wear their literary influences lightly. Having said this, I'm equally sure the opposite *isn't* true. Literature can and should aspire to a musical condition.

This is what struck me most forcefully as I sat around in grad school, hunting and pecking: how unafraid musicians were, the tremendous passionate rights they granted themselves. Forget exposition, backstory, the polite accretion of detail. They were in it for the impact. They wanted to *fuck their fans up.* Whereas us writers were left to toil in private, emptying ourselves onto blank pages and hoping someday our efforts might take root inside anonymous readers. We were emotional sperm donors. Was I seeing things a bit too dramatically? Well, of course I was; I was a graduate student.

Graduation rid me of that privilege, but I remained inflamed by futility. To help matters along, I moved to a new city and wrote an eight-hundred-page novel about sixteenth-century Jewish mysticism, despite knowing nothing about the time period or topic. This tome took nearly two years to complete and put everyone I know to sleep. It was all quite prog.

Joe Henry remained my role model. I still wanted to be able to tell stories the way he did, without bitterness or histrionics. Only I didn't have melody or rhythm at my disposal. It felt hopeless. Then, one day, I was sitting around trying to write and failing and feeling sorry for myself and listening to Joe and this one line popped out of the speaker: *Here comes the rapture of song and story.* And this made me think of the opening line of the *Iliad*, which goes, *Sing, Goddess, the anger of Peleus' son Achilles and its devastation.* And this made me think of the lyric soliloquy delivered by Reverend Hightower in Faulkner's *Light in August.* The connection in my head being that all language began in song and that the best stories inevitably return to song, to a state of rapture. For years, I had assumed that throwing beautiful words at the page would make my prose feel true. But I had the process exactly backward. It was truth that lifted the language into beauty and toward song.

It was a matter of doing what Joe Henry did, of pursuing characters into moments of emotional truth and *slowing down.* The result was a compression of sensual and psychological detail that released the rhythm and melody in language itself, what Longfellow called "the happy accidents of language." I wouldn't have recognized it then, but I was trying to identify the process by which a writer might sing.

Our Song

It was Joe Henry who had triggered this epiphany, so I took the logical next step, abusing my marginal status as a "music journalist" to finagle an interview. It was my idea that Joe and I were going to become great friends, a dependable delusion among Fanatics. Well, I got the interview, anyway.

And then something totally unprecedented happened: A few summers ago I received a remarkable e-mail from Mr. Henry. He knew me to be a writer and therefore attached a poem he'd composed on July 4th, asking if I "had any thoughts." I did have a thought. *Holy shit,* I thought, *Joe Henry just sent me something to read.*

The opening stanza described Willie Mays shopping for garage door openers at a Home Depot in Scottsdale, Arizona. I loved it, the unlikely collision of the archetypal and mundane. Then something unfortunate happened; the poem's pathos sputtered into rage. There was a lot about how stupid Americans are. Red Bull was cited, as were the ravages of global warming. I was reminded (unpleasantly) of my own writing. And thus my next thought: I'm going to have to tell Joe Henry that *his poem kind of sucks.*

By the time I'd composed my critique Joe had rewritten the poem and set it to music. He e-mailed me a demo of the song, just piano and voice. In its somber beauty, it called to mind Woody Guthrie's "This Land Is Your Land," the dream of America as a holy wilderness whose decline is properly understood as a cause for lamentation, not sermons.

Willie Mays was no longer being deployed as a frothing symbol of America's greatness gone to lard. He had become a spokesman for the spiritual reckoning that would have to precede any national redemption. "This was my country," he observed,

This was my song
Somewhere in the middle there
Though it started badly and it's ending wrong.
This was God's country,
This frightful and this angry land
But if it's His will the worst of it might still
Somehow make me a better man

I now venture the following absurd claim: that this song, its very manner of composition, prophesied the end of the Bush Era, the false dream of aggression as salvation, the tireless denials and indecent projections of evil, and the beginning of the Obama Era, in its humility, in its bruised optimism and Afro-Christian evocations. I am not suggesting that Joe Henry set out to do anything other than express his deepest concerns. Only that these concerns were, to a startling degree, shared by his fellow citizens, as subsequent events would affirm.

This is what artists do, actually—as the pundits fizz away in their bright studios, narrating our civic fate like a form of athletic combat—they transcribe the individual heart seeking a collective conscience, a reason to believe. You can certainly think of me as a sap for making such a grandiose statement, but listen to the song first.

A Very Low Bar

I kept trying to find excuses to interview Joe Henry again. I wanted to know more about how he composed his lyrics and whether he'd ever written fiction and whether he'd be willing to ghostwrite mine. We never got that far. But in the spring of 2008 Joe did agree to appear on a panel I'd organized in Los Angeles about the relationship between literature and songwriting. He suggested inviting his friend Aimee, who was also a musician. Aimee Mann, he meant.

"Cool," I said, as calmly as I could.

Mann was everything I expected: smart, funny, gorgeous, and high-strung. A decade ago, I would have developed a raging crush on her, just for the sake of humiliating myself. But our panel had been scheduled for Sunday morning at the very rock and roll hour of 10:30 a.m. Aimee did not appear amused. I glanced down at my list of questions and quietly scratched out the one suggested by a friend: *Can you talk about the symbolic undercarriage of the line, "Hush hush, keep it down now, voices carry"?*

The most fascinating thing about the panel, for me, was that Aimee Mann felt intimidated talking about songwriting next to Joe

Henry. She went so far as to scoff at her reputation as a literary song-writer: "You mention that someone's drinking coffee and it's a Tues-day and suddenly you're a genius. It's a very low bar."

Without exactly meaning to, she drove the point home by perform-ing "Freeway," the single from her album @ #%&*! Smilers. The song was a wry character sketch of the suburban wastrels who populate Southern California. Then Joe got up to sing "This Afternoon," a track from 2003's Tiny Voices. The difference was impossible to miss.

Joe's tale was told by a teenage prostitute in Havana who described his life on the afternoon Fidel Castro's rebels captured the city. The details were precise and indelibly sad. The song cast the upheavals of history as a backdrop to the personal corruptions we endure. It was a Graham Greene novel, basically, set to soul music.

Am I suggesting that Joe's song was "better" than Aimee's? Nope. The crowd enjoyed "Freeway" far more than "This Afternoon." It had a catchier hook and chorus. It trafficked in the simple pleasures we expect from a pop song. And by *simple* I don't mean dumb; I mean accessible.

What I am suggesting is that Joe's song was trying to transport us, trying to make us imagine what it would be like to be another human being. Aimee Mann doesn't do that kind of work. She casts a gimlet eye on the world and offers her fans an "Aimee Mann song." This is her solution to the crisis of sentiment: she assumes an ironic posture that protects her from excessive feeling.

Joe's solution is more complicated. He wants to impart deep feel-ing, but he doesn't want anyone to get the idea that he's blabbering about his heart. So he invents a world where he can safely project his emotional concerns. This is the essential impulse of a fiction writer.

As I listened to the two of them, I got to thinking more broadly about the relationship between lyrics and artistic influence. The top of the charts will always be the preserve of those who voice the old tropes with conviction. *Since my baby left me and I'm crazy for loving you and I want to rock and roll all night.* There was a time, before the rise of television and videos, when stars like Dylan or the Beatles made hits out of fictional creation. But today's stars are much more like brands. Their personas—lovesick, nubile, wounded, enigmatic, whatever it is—have become the central product in all their songs.

There are plenty of reasons Joe Henry hasn't become a household name. His songs run six minutes and often involve jazz musicians. But the main thing is his lyrics. Whatever marketable persona he might present remains too submerged in his art. The same is true of Tom Waits, for instance, or Randy Newman. These guys are like brilliant short story writers living in an era of celebrity memoir. And I'm not sure this is a bad thing.

The crowd at the panel had come out to hear Aimee Mann. She was the star attraction. But this fact made her seem oddly trapped: she had to be Aimee Mann. There was no room for surprise. Whereas, right at the end, when Joe got up and began to perform "Our Song," a sense of wonder rippled through that auditorium. There was one woman in the front row whose face was alight. She had no idea who Joe Henry was. She knew only that she was going somewhere she hadn't been before, and he was taking her there.

10

The Mating Habits of the Drooling Fanatic

A certain Elise —— invited me to visit her upstate. We had met two months earlier at a literary event and instantly sensed in the other the avid temperament of the orgasmically needy. A series of quivering phone calls ensued. Elise had the dewy gaze of a Bollywood heroine and the relentless pep of a midwestern football mascot. I wanted to defile her. I wanted her to defile me. I wanted public gymnastics capped by a naked perp walk. If all that went well, we could get hitched and coauthor the Sex Addict Memoir.

This was during my era of Dismal Blind Dates (1997–2004) and I saw no reason to behave responsibly. I was still living in Somerville and scraping by as an Adjunct Professor of Bitterness. So I flew out to a writer's conference near the college where she taught; that was how we rigged things. I stayed at her place rather than some hotel because why-not-save-the-money plus she-had-plenty-of-room. For two days we knocked around town, gobbling fried fish and trying to figure out how to jump-start the defiling process. At night we lay in our respective rooms, broiling in cowardice. The tension was idiotic and throbbing and awesome.

On morning three I woke up determined to act. I took a shower and slathered deodorant on my junk and when I walked out of her bathroom the stereo was blaring. The only way I can describe the music is to say it was mall-friendly, soft, synthesized, entirely devout in its stunted emotional ambitions.

"Who is this?" I said.

"Air Supply!" Elise said.

I searched her tender face for the slightest trace of irony.

"This is their *Greatest Hits*," she said.

I closed my eyes and nodded. It seemed important that I not say anything snide. My mind lunged about for possible Air Supply repartee. The only thing that came to mind was a high school soccer practice where Jon Carnoy mentioned Air Supply and Dave Andersen and Danny Luotto started chanting "Fag Supply!" in what they took to be Australian accents.

And how were Air Supply doing after all these years? They were *all out of love*. They were *making love out of nothing at all*. They were (more broadly) *lost in love*.

If you are now thinking I rebuffed Elise because of her fondness for Air Supply, think again, friend. After seventy-two hours spent marinating in lust, you could not have stopped my dick with a Taser. When the time finally came, we auditioned numerous panting configurations, with much attendant grind and slurp.

The problem arose, as it so often does, upon reflection. Elise was supposed to be everything I wanted: brilliant, delectable, willing. But as I returned to Boston, as I furiously throttled myself to the memory of her haunches, my mind kept fixing on Air Supply. I kept seeing Russell Hitchcock in his lacquered mulletfro. Worse, I kept hearing his voice. *Don't know which way to turn,* he keened. *Don't know which boat to burn.* Right, I thought. The multiple boats. The bloody indecision over which to burn.

Did I honestly believe Elise lacked the emotional depth required to be involved with me? Was this even possible? Indeed, wasn't my willingness to dismiss this woman based solely on her earnest devotion to a soft rock duo proof of my own spiritual disfigurement?

In a word: possibly.

In fact, my reaction neatly encapsulates the romantic inclinations of the Drooling Fanatic. I could see, based on the Air Supply situation, that Elise and I were susceptible to different myths. Hers were starry-eyed and operatic, full of blond people in Members Only jackets necking on tarmacs. Mine were shadowy and downbeat and involved horny Communists engaged in light bondage. There was some chance our myths might overlap in the arena of depravity. (Perhaps the Communists were blond; perhaps the bondage could be staged on a tarmac.) But soon enough, Elise would be sighing a lot and asking why I listened to such sad music all the time. Did I have something against just being happy? And I'd be gouging up her Air Supply records, then blaming it on her dog.

I Fucked a Drooling Fanatic and All I Got Was This Lousy Mixed CD

Be it resolved: We are not easy people to love. We spend too much time listening to our music, explaining why our music is so brilliant, resenting those who neglect our music, and hating ourselves because we can't make music. Our less obvious offenses include:

1. Inept Rites of Seduction Anyone who has dated a Drooling Fanatic can recall the painful moment when it becomes apparent that he (or less often she) is going to try to use music to compensate for deficits of charm, intellect, and sexual prowess. You can safely conjure the usual mood-setting clichés—soft lighting, red wine, incense—as our Fanatic makes his way to the stereo, poorly pretending his musical selection is happenstance when he has spent the past week (at least) worrying the aphrodisiacal merits of Miles Davis's *Kind of Blue* versus Sinatra's *In the Wee Small Hours*.

This is assuming the best. For Drooling Fanatics are unfailingly blind to the liabilities of their own taste. I have subjected would-be lovers to such loin-parching classics as Tesla's *Five Man Acoustical Jam*, Johnny Cash's *At Folsom Prison*, and, on one dire occasion, *The Murder Ballads*. (If you have not yet attempted to remove a woman's camisole with Nick Cave croaking, "I'm a bad motherfucker, don't you know, but I'll crawl over fifty good pussies just to get one fat boy's ass-hole" in the background, you haven't quite lived.)

Even when Drooling Fanatics get the tunes right, there is a lurking danger. Rather than attending to the unfolding carnal drama, we become preoccupied by the soundtrack. We begin to wonder if our dates are listening carefully enough. "Wait, wait," we say, "you have to hear *this* part," and "They use a moog when they play this song live" and "Can you believe it? A *moog*!" and pretty soon our date is yawning and saying how she needs to get some sleep, she's got to vacuum out her car the next morning.

2. Sonic Presumptions But okay, let's say you're the patient type. You find our enthusiasm endearing. You mistake our fanaticism for passion. For whatever reason, you get involved with us. Congratulations! You will now be subjected—more or less constantly—to the ridiculous bigotries so integral to the Drooling Fanatic self-esteem complex. We will squint at your CDs and when you ask why, we'll say, "Oh no, nothing, I just didn't realize Pearl Jam was still together." We will help "revamp" your iTunes library, perhaps without your consent. We will drag you to shows in venues where hope has died. We will do this because we are dickheads. But the sad part is we're not even trying to be dickheads. It's just that music is the central expression of who we are, how *we* hope to be judged, and now that we're together, well, you're a part of that too, babe. If you possess a CD by the Spin

Doctors, we feel it is incumbent upon us to rescue you. We know you're a better person than that, deeper, more authentic. It's like we're getting you off drugs.

3. A Perpetual Effort to Colonize   Life with a Drooling Fanatic probably won't require a new address (our place is kind of cluttered) or a new set of friends (we don't have many), but it will require a new musical sensibility. Because it's not just a matter of getting you off your drugs. You've also got to get on ours.

Back in my El Paso years, for instance, I became obsessed with an album called *Road Apples* by the Canadian band the Tragically Hip. The music was rock by way of the Stones, overwrought electric blues, and I played it constantly. I was living over a grocery store owned by a pair of Lebanese brothers and when I came downstairs for a box of Pop-Tarts, I often could hear one of them murmuring *culled and wooed, bitten, chewed, baby it won't hurt if you don't move* in a glottal Arab accent.

Then my girlfriend moved in with me. She was a fan of Cannonball Adderley and Touré Kunda, artists who, like her, exuded a terrifying sophistication. I pummeled her with *Road Apples*. Pummeled as she cooked gourmet meals involving sherry and shallots, as we humped with eager, postcollegiate ineptitude, as she slept. My girlfriend came to like the Hip. She overlooked the band's idiotic name and limited range. But she couldn't bring herself to love them as I did and eventually moved out. There were, as Princess Di might have put it, three of us in the relationship.

Or consider (once again) The Close. Not only did he spend the entirety of his courtship dragging his intended to White Stripes shows, not only did he somewhat creepily begin appropriating the wardrobe of Jack White (posters of whom high-schoolishly plastered every square inch of his apartment) but he insisted their wedding party have a "White Stripes theme," meaning everyone had to dress in black and white and red.. He did not force his bride to sit behind a drum kit, though I'm sure he lobbied.

I think we can all agree such behavior reflects rampant egocentrism. But there's an even more virulent fantasy at work, I'm afraid. Drooling Fanatics honestly believe that if you come to love our music, you will love us. You will understand the exalted suffering and luminous desire we can't ever quite articulate. Which brings us to . . .

4. Our Reliance on Songs to Access Our Emotional Lives Here, it might be best to cite the pop culture touchstone of Drooling Fanaticism— the scene from the film *Say Anything*[13] in which John Cusack stands across the street from Ione Skye's bedroom with a boom box over his head blaring Snoop Dogg's timeless classic "Bitches Ain't Shit."

Wait. Check that. According to Wikipedia, he's actually playing "In Your Eyes" by Peter Gabriel. Fine.

So this was how people serenaded each other back in the 1980s. But it begs the question: is this the best you can do, John Cusack character guy? Romeo scales a wall. Cyrano praises Roxanne's lilies. Even Don Giovanni, pretty much the ultimate scumbag of all opera, sings Elvira an aria. The Drooling Fanatic has neither courage nor talents of self-expression at his disposal. Thus, we must rely on our playlists to speak for us.

In the early stages of courtship—as, say, on the brink of a first kiss—I cue up tracks that announce *I am painfully sensitive and will love you till the end of time.* "I Was Just Thinking" by Teitur is a lock. As matters proceed, the compositions should suggest mysterious, possibly agitated, depths of feeling, the basic message being *I have been wounded and remain frightened you will wound me, but it might help if*

---

13. The 1989 film about a lovesick dude who ardently woos an unattainable love object using a vintage New Wave soundtrack, stumbles into some vague form of self-knowledge, and thereby gets the girl. I believe I have just described every single character John Cusack has ever played.

you take off your blouse. "Every Little Bit Hurts" by Paul Thorn works well. As for the serious business, I'm a proponent of songs that combine abject female body worship and a vigorous rhythm section (ideally "Pretty Brown Skin" by Roy Ayers).

But this is just me, of course, the same guy who once considered Nick Cave suitable foreplay. I would never deign to DJ someone else's thunderdome. To do so would violate what I have come to think of as the Porno Parallax. To wit: If you've ever watched amateur pornography, you will have noticed that many of the videos, sort of unwittingly, capture the music playing in the room at the time. And thus, those of us who make the admittedly poor decision to watch amateur pornography must endure, along with poor lighting and ill-advised genital grooming, scraps of Quarterflash's "Harden My Heart" or Riskay's "Smell Yo Dick." Not songs that *I* associate with erotic reverie, but presumably the very ones the lovers in question selected to inspire them to perform sexual acts on camera.

5. *Drooling Fanatics Struggle in Social Settings* Of course we do. That's us, by the way, hovering next to the dip. And no, we don't know what's in it that makes it so tasty. We're busy mulling the music—what it is, whether it meets our standards, how we might seize control of the stereo. Indeed, the relational style of the Drooling Fanatic at a party might best be summarized as Asperger's with a Backbeat.

Unless, of course, two Drooling Fanatics encounter each other, in which case you can bank on an initial period of excitement, the swapping of multiple band names and at least one protracted spat. The writer Brock Clarke and I once argued for three hours in a bar in Clemson, South Carolina, over which was a more "important" band, Pavement (his pick) or Los Lobos (mine). I very much admire Brock's work and like him as a person. But when I think about his defense of this idiotic premise I pity him. I am certain he feels the same way toward me.

Becca's Song

Am I overstating the emotional incapacities of Drooling Fanatics?
Probably. Very few of us say the things we should to the people we
love. We find other ways to reach our deepest feelings. Drooling
Fanatics just happen to use music.

A case in point: I can remember staring out of my Toyota Tercel at
snow tapering onto the low hills of East Tennessee while my pal
Becca Moore sat in the passenger seat close to tears. I wasn't the cause
of her unhappiness. That distinction belonged to another guy, who'd
moved in with Becca and led her to believe they might get married
before reverting to the habits of his given species, the North American Bachelor Chicken.

I'd spent some happy nights with Becca, getting wasted and listening to music and gobbling the grease bombs you can afford to gobble
when you're twenty-five. I was screwing around with a friend of hers,
a sexy divorcée I had no intention of marrying because I was a North
American Bachelor Chicken too. Then Becca's Chicken broke her
heart and she called me one night to say she needed to get out of
town, bad, and should we do a road trip.

The snow struck us both as overkill. Then a road crew appeared
and began tearing up our half of the highway and traffic drew to a
dead halt. This felt like a bad metaphor, the kind that yearned for a
home in one of my short stories.

Becca gazed at the snow. She was no weeper. Relentless optimism
was more her style. She'd come tearing out of Indiana and built herself into a fearsome capitalist. She was like a lot of women I knew
back then: brash in public, and quietly terrified in private. Her apartment was piled high with cross-stitch patterns and photo albums of
other people's children. And now she was staring thirty in the kisser,
alone.

Then James McMurtry came on my stereo and the first words out of his mouth were (I shit you not) *Must be a cold front coming / 'cause I saw the eastbound C&O / And the coal cars were dusted with a half inch of snow.* This was "Rachel's Song," the saddest four minutes released in that whole godforsaken year of 1996. I'd always assumed the song was narrated by a young widow driven to madness by mourning. But I heard it differently now. It wasn't about death but romantic abandonment, the terrible shame of being left behind, which caused Becca to break down once and for all, to weep convulsively, because she was a Drooling Fanatic, like her ex, they had both loved McMurtry, and because songs held this power over her, they could make her feel the grief she wanted to feel and didn't want to feel. The song ended and Becca wiped her eyes. "That was ridiculous," she said, and began searching the map for alternative routes.

I certainly knew what it meant to be haunted by a record. For me, that year, it was Howard Tate's searing soul masterpiece, *Get It While You Can,* which I played at absurd volumes, burning through one chintzy tweeter after another. Tate was the classic sob story, a singer revered by the pros and stiffed by the paying customers. His heyday was in the late sixties but he was gone a few years later, leaving behind only his voice: angelic, confused, convincingly aggrieved. He kept getting mixed up with the wrong ladies, beaten down by those bad broads. That falsetto! I was sure he'd been sent to rescue me.

Then I met a girl, and another aspect of Tate's music was revealed to me. It was a kind of sexual tonic. Those honeyed horn charts. Those crisp drums and opulent organ riffs. When sprinkled over young lovers, the result was prolonged necking, very sleek frottage. We were dead in love for a month, bruising each other up in the sack, whispering the sweet lies of infatuation. It all curdled quickly enough and she began to tromp around town with my best friend. Howard Tate understood. All of his songs were about betrayal.

On those nights when I made the mistake of drink, I would stagger home and lie on the bathroom floor and listen to the tinkling piano of the title track, the mournful horns. Then Tate would start in: "When you love somebody, you take a chance on sorrow . . ." and soon I would be mumbling into her answering machine, asking her did she remember the time we did it during that snowstorm, how the window was open and my feet went numb with snowflakes?

This is typical Drooling Fanatic behavior. As much as we might enjoy romance and its attendant dramas, we're really just waiting for the versions of love that return to us later, in song.

Reluctant Exegesis:
"All Out of Love"

Dedicated to those readers who find the previously cited conduct toward Elise immature, bordering on disreputable.

I'm lying alone with my head on the phone
Thinking of you till it hurts
I know you hurt too but what else can we do
Tormented and torn apart

What I love so much about the soft rock ballad (SRB), and what makes it the musical equivalent of the romance novel, is that the words make sense *until you actually focus on them*. The first line presents a lovesick narrator who is "alone" and "on the phone," a situation common to narrators of SRBs. But look again. The narrator's head is actually *on* a phone.

The year is 1980, so we're talking about a large plastic device, possibly of the rotary genus. This act presumably mirrors, or serves as a masochistic expression of, the narrator's anguish. He now addresses the object of his love. He acknowledges that she is also in pain.

(Perhaps her head is on a phone as well.) These two represent an ancient archetype: star-crossed lovers. Powerful forces have intervened. They are Abelard and Héloïse, Romeo and Juliet, Britney and K-Fed.

I wish I could carry your smile in my heart
For times when my life feels so low
It would make me believe what tomorrow could bring
When today doesn't really know, doesn't really know

The listener grows concerned. Having been informed of the epic forces aligned against our lovers, we are eager to discern their exact nature and potential remedy. Instead, the narrator reiterates his devotion. He concludes with a couplet that calls to mind Heidegger's ultimate declaration in *Being and Time* (*Sein und Zeit*, 1927): "a primordial mode of temporalizing of ecstatic temporality itself must make the ecstatic project of being in general possible." Translation: your smile, my heart, let's roll.

I'm all out of love, I'm so lost without you
I know you were right believing for so long
I'm all out of love, what am I without you
I can't be too late to say that I was so wrong

The chorus has arrived. With it, our hope for clarity evaporates. We have been proceeding under the assumption that our lovers were somehow "torn apart." We now discover what actually tore them apart: the narrator. He dumped her. More precisely, he dumped her after a long period of emotional neglect.

I want you to come back and carry me home
Away from these long lonely nights
I'm reaching for you, are you feeling it too
Does the feeling seem oh so right

The problem is one of credibility. The speaker is playing the part of a victim when he is clearly the assailant. We must now endure his entreaties. He wants her to "come back and carry me home" (huh?) not because he recognizes in her precious qualities he once neglected, but because he's lonely. Love in the realm of Air Supply is a lot like shock and awe: an overwhelming force that erases any trace of moral responsibility. What matters is that your head is on a phone and it kind of hurts because phones are hard and this pain is reflected in your voice, you are digging deep into your man-pain, you are truly coming clean, you are saying for the whole bloody world to hear, My bad, babe.

And what would you say if I called on you now
And said that I can't hold on
There's no easy way, it gets harder each day
Please love me or I'll be gone, I'll be gone

Having already lied and groveled, our hero now turns to the next refuge of the abusive boyfriend: guilt provocation. If his ex, whom he dumped, refuses to love him, he will kill himself. Or maybe by "gone" he means only that he'll abandon her (again). Regardless, he has established a clear pattern of deceit, obsession, and unsolicited contact that seems predictive of assault. It's time for the bridge.

Oh, what are you thinking of?
What are you thinking of?
Oh, what are you thinking of?
What are you thinking of?

I'm thinking about Elise again, actually. I'm thinking about how she knew the words to all the Air Supply songs she played for me. And I'm thinking about the fact that 98 percent of the people who listen to Air Supply are women and how much they must enjoy hearing men "express their feelings" and plead for forgiveness—even when those men are poised to inflict more damage. As in the romance novel or the Lifetime Channel original movie, the SRB peddles women a version of love that manages to hold them in contempt. It comes on like surrender and delivers abuse.

But I'm also thinking (again) about the broader relationship between language and music, how melody and rhythm can animate dead language, which is on the one hand beautiful and inspiring and on the other hand disturbing, to have all these dead words stumbling the earth like zombies in makeup. And I'm thinking that this is what it's like for me to hear "All Out of Love." It's like a zombie in mascara wants to bite my neck, a slow clumsy zombie but one with terrific stamina, as is so often the case with zombies, meaning eventually I have to sleep, or I trip over something I wouldn't usually trip over, and the zombie gets close enough to chomp through my skin, and when that happens I don't die, but the part of my brain that regards language as an instrument of truth dies, the part that does the honest work of investigating romantic ruin, the hows and whys of the emotional harm we do one another, and instead of feeling nauseated by "All Out of Love" I get choked up and try to sing along, which is when my friends realize what's happened and put a bullet in my brain.

The Marriage of Fanatico

It is fair to ask at this point how I ever managed to get married. That is certainly a question my family has pondered. A proper librettist— or perhaps Air Supply—would have drawn it up perfectly: my wife, Erin, and I locking eyes across a windswept piazza, plenty of loud obstacles in the wings (a dastardly count, a mischievous ghost, a buxom romantic rival capable of nailing high C). Alas, the truth is a bit lumpier. But I'll start at the beginning, because our courtship only survived by the good graces of our Fanaticism.

Act I: An Immodest Proposal

In April 2002, my first book came out, a collection of stories. I was thirty-five years old, seven summers removed from grad school, and so desperate for regard that I would have approved the title *Stupid Things My Penis Has Done*. The publisher settled on *My Life in Heavy Metal*.

Already, there was a bit of operatic fortune at work, because my future wife happened to be a former metal chick with literary aspirations. The only reason she came to my debut reading was because of this title. There she was on the appointed night, a shy woman with dark hair and sad blue eyes, though I wouldn't have noticed her because the venue—a tiny bar in Cambridge—was hot and packed. Erin kept having to step outside to clear her head. She left before I even started.

After the reading, Erin's friend Kate approached me and told me about Erin falling ill and mentioned that their book club was reading my stories and I immediately volunteered to visit. I was all about chivalry that might get me laid. The book club visit turned out pretty awkward. Of the five members, the most vocal was an ill-tempered lesbian doctor who clearly hated the book. Erin said very little, but she did mention that she was a writer, and naturally I urged her to call me for advice.

A couple of nights later my phone rang. Erin wanted to say thanks, and to take me up on my offer. She had some stories she needed feedback on. I told her that I'd love to read one, but I was up to my neck in student stories.

"You're missing out," she said.

"I'm sure I am," I said. "Maybe you could read one to me sometime."

She paused. "Sure."

"What would you be wearing at this reading?" I said.

"I'd be naked, of course."

Erin was trying to sound casual, as if this were the sort of proposal she dispensed with some frequency. But her voice fluttered and both of us could feel, in the flushed half-second afterward, the abrupt acceleration of our pulses. Whatever it was we'd been up to previously, the real purpose of her call had been revealed.

Act II: Drooling Consummation

Erin showed up Saturday night and I fed her linguine with homemade vodka sauce and sweet white wine. We were both terrified by the audacity of what she'd promised. For all her bravado, Erin was a modest woman. And I myself, despite having published a book so graphic that a cousin of mine felt it necessary to transport it in a brown paper bag, despite the inevitable reputation this book saddled me with, remained crushingly insecure. The idea that a beautiful woman had shown up at my apartment prepared to remove her clothing flummoxed me. In my experience you had to do a lot of pleading before anything like that happened.

It was soon apparent that the bottle we'd drained at dinner was not going to see us through to the main event. We needed help. And so I led Erin into the sunroom and put on the sexiest record I could think of, Joe Henry's *Fuse*, and waited to see how Erin would react to its narcotic drum loops. We wound up slow dancing.

"What is this *music*?" Erin whispered, which you must know by now is the question every Fanatic yearns to be asked.

So I told her about Joe Henry, about how *Fuse* was his finest record, how I'd nearly wept when I found six copies in the ninety-nine-cent bin at Disc Diggers, how I'd bought every one and sent them to friends with a note reading *Please allow me to save your life*, how *Fuse* had convinced Ornette Coleman to work with Joe on his next album. Then I played her Coleman's solo, which lasts just over a minute and transforms the blues scale into something more like a dream state. It was like having someone brush their fingertips along the pleasure center of our brains. Erin showed her lovely crooked smile. Her body unclenched, then swayed.

But there was this other matter to attend to, so Erin marched into my bedroom and shut the door. *The king-sized bed. The dark wainscoting. The chocolates scattered about.* What must she have thought? It was all quite dismal. To her eternal credit, she undressed anyway and slipped under the covers and I walked in and her pale shoulders were blazing. She read me a story about a repressed nun who lusts after her star pupil. Then I stripped and read her a story about a vegetarian woman who lusts after a steak. Then it was time for the hot blood to do its work.

Act III: A Summertime Thing

Why did I sit Erin down a mere two weeks later and announce that we had to stop seeing each other? Because my superego had decided I needed to find a wife, and while my superego had not bothered to inform my slobbering id, it had made a pretty convincing case against Erin who, for all her charms, was twenty-seven and just a few years out of college. I looked at her life—the damp apartment, the corporate job, the quotes from famous writers taped above her desk—and saw a prettier version of myself a decade earlier. It felt tawdry and maybe even a little ruthless to lead her on.

And so I bid her farewell, convinced I'd behaved with noble restraint, and returned to my alleged quest for a bride. It turned out there was a whole army of us out there, men and women in our mid-thirties, zooming around our big cities in bright cars with lousy suspension. We met online and through friends and at parties and grinned desperately and poured our life stories out over artichoke dip. We waited for Cupid to hurry up already and shoot us in the ass so we could start having all those kids we were supposed to want.

I drove an hour through the snow to meet one woman. We'd made sexy talk on the phone and swapped photos. It was going to be tremendous. (It was always going to be tremendous.) Then she opened the door and her face was that of an ostrich, pinched and belligerent, and mine was that of a weasel, beady and mean, and our hearts staggered through the rest of it, the hope punched out of us.

It was on such nights, a little later than was appropriate, that I dialed Erin's number. "I've got something you need to hear," I'd say, which was deplorable but at least true because when I wasn't off turning dates into Bergman films, all I did was hunt for new dope. And so

Erin appeared and we retreated into my cave and did what was required, all the sweaty investigations, though best of all was lying in the dark afterward and listening to the songs that were—unbeknownst to either of us, I think—slowly twining our fates.

I played her *Lovers Knot* by Jeb Loy Nichols and *Living with Ghosts* by Patty Griffin and *Rabbit Songs* by Hem and *The Sons of Intemperance Offering* by Phil Cody and *Everybody's Got Their Something* by Nikka Costa. We ate French toast in great abundance and slept as if dead. After a few weeks, I'd break up with her, though sometimes she broke up with me, coming to her senses with a soft reluctance while I nodded soberly.

But then the new Chuck Prophet album came out, *No Other Love* it was called, and I knew Erin would want to hear it. She was as nuts about Chuck as I was, as gaga for his Southern California drawl and the sticky-sweet sorrow of his melodies, as aroused by his languid arrangements. "I know we're broken up," I said. "But you're not going to believe this record."

This was the summer of 2003 as I recall and we spent the next week doing nothing but listening in bed, until we knew all the words and the tempos had been absorbed by our muscles and every song seemed to be trying to tell us something new about our dire arrangement. It was the perfect record for us, gorgeous and doomed, like a kiss that tastes of blood, and the song we took as our anthem was "Summertime Thing," which we sang to each other and to ourselves, dancing across the dirty floors of my apartment naked and bracing ourselves against the relevant countertops. Erin knew she shouldn't have allowed herself to get sucked back into my orbit, and I couldn't tell her otherwise. So there were some fresh tears, and when it was all over, well, to quote Chuck, "We snuck off like thieves, with our backs to each other."

Act IV: Bad Babysitter

This is how it goes when the DF is falling in love, especially when he doesn't know, or won't admit, he's falling in love. It's not the lightning bolt or the sunset embrace. It's the way she infiltrates your most sacred LPs, quietly erases the y from your collection. And so, while it's true that Erin and I were never officially "together," and while I insisted to all who would listen that Erin was not "the one" because I was looking for a wife (dammit), one powerful enough to compensate for the many inadequacies I would bring to the marriage—by which I mean some kind of magical mommy/whore/nurse figure who would ravage me then bear my children and mother them with effortless expertise, all while subsidizing my writing career and keeping my blue moods at bay—while all this was true, pathetically, inexorably, it was also true that, by the spring of 2004, most of the albums I loved made me think of Erin.

Then Chuck Prophet came to town (at last) and I got two tickets and gave them both to Erin, which I saw as an act of generosity because I'm just that stupid. We were really and truly broken up. And Erin was enough of a Fanatic, God bless her, to take those tickets and push her way to the front of the crowd, because Chuck, it turned out, could *shred*. She called to tell me about it that same night and we both imagined each other naked and agreed how it was great we could still be friends.

Then Erin mentioned something else: she'd been accepted into an MFA program in Southern California, one of the most prestigious in the country. I was happy for her, overjoyed really because now that she was leaving, I mean, what was the harm in getting in a few last licks?

That was the summer of Cee-Lo Green and The Sleepy Jackson and Princess Superstar, whose song "Bad Babysitter" captured the moral depths to which we aspired. This was just another idyll, because I didn't believe in long-distance relationships, and that was fine with Erin, she wasn't looking for a husband. So there was no big scene when she left that fall. I sent her off in her little Honda with enough mixed CDs to survive the big square states.

We missed each other more than we let on. Speaking for myself, I learned to avoid certain records in certain moods, though often I listened to them anyway. If I found a new record that I knew was going to be special, I would sometimes try to guess which songs Erin would like. Later, around bedtime, I'd call her and play them over the phone.

I continued to go on dates. That winter, I took out a doctor. Smart, attractive—Jewish even! We got back to her apartment and I began rooting around for her record collection. "Where's your music?" I said casually.

"Oh," she said. "My schedule is pretty hectic."

"But right now," I said. "We could listen to something right now."

She smiled, a little indulgently, as if to say, *I don't know how it is with you writers, but this is how it is with us doctors,* though what she said was maybe worse: "I think I've got a Sade disc in my car."

And so I found myself at home again, in the familiar rooms, and though I knew it was a mistake I put on one of Erin's favorites, *Post-cards from Downtown* by Dayna Kurtz, a collection of songs so full of romantic woe it might as well have come with a bottle of whiskey. And I was doing okay, really, until the moment, four and a half minutes into her rueful epic "Paterson," when the song seems to be drawing to an end, and instead, the time signature slows and we hear the trill of an accordion and violins and plucked guitar and Dayna begins singing in Italian of all things—*Oh mio coure!*—over and over, and listening to this voice echo about my bedroom, its unending dejection, made me realize that keeping Erin at bay was no longer an option, that my loneliness was not some precious artistic prerogative or exalted state but simply an ongoing regret. I needed her in close now, where we could hear the music together.[14]

Interlude:
The Kip Winger Canon

Erin and I were lying in bed, stoned, when she started in again about her "single days," which is a special code phrase she uses when she wants to remind me about the time Kip Winger nearly propositioned her.

This took place during Erin's first year in grad school. She'd been invited by an old friend to a VH1-sponsored event, which combined the channel's parasitic passion for aging celebrities with its ongoing campaign to resuscitate the music of the eighties. Many of Erin's hair metal heroes were on hand to support the guest of honor, Jani Lane, the former lead singer of Warrant, who was struggling to mount a comeback.

It is fair to suppose Erin was lonely. It is fair to suppose she had a few drinks, and that these drinks helped steer her into the seat next to Kip Winger at the table where the musicians were signing merchandise for fans. Many of these fans were (and I quote) "slutty girls with their tits hanging out" whose sexual availability was understood. But to hear Erin tell it, Kip hadn't been interested in them.

To hear Erin tell it, Kip had been interested in Erin. It pleased Erin a great deal to be the object of Kip Winger's lewd banter, and it pleased

14. Did I therefore propose to my beloved on some windswept piazza? Not exactly. Instead, I knocked her up over winter break and we eloped three months later, as she was finishing grad school. I announced all this good news to her parents, grinning idiotically as her mother spiraled into an aria of silent rage. It was pure opera, that moment, raw and woeful, and Erin's mother had every right to kill me, particularly after I made the inexplicable decision to show her the "unofficial" wedding photos, in which Erin is half-naked and I am brandishing a bottle of Jack Daniel's.

Yes, I realize I'm a dipshit.

her to be able to report to me the next day, on the phone, that she had been the object of Kip Winger's lewd banter and that he had discussed oral sex and implied his expertise and stopped just short of inviting her back to his hotel room to prove his claim. Or maybe he had invited her. It was impossible to know what happened, and she enjoyed this ambiguity also.

So this was her Kip Winger Story and she was telling it to me once again, now that we were old married farts with a kid sacked out across the hall. The pot had made her nostalgic. Then she started in with certain Facts About Kip mentioned in previous tellings, such as the fact that Kip had studied ballet and could kick his foot over his head while wearing leather trousers. Kip had studied classical music and composition. Kip was not a tall man, but he had aged superbly. Then she got online and showed me a YouTube video of Kip playing classical guitar in leather trousers.

This was, technically, our date night.

"I guess I didn't realize that Kip Winger was such a Renaissance man," I said. "There's probably a whole genre of literature devoted to Kip."

"That's right," Erin said. "There is. It's called Kip Lit."

"Wow," I said.

"*Kip Flew over the Cuckoo's Nest*," she said. "Just for instance."

"How's that one go?"

"Kip's ballet moves are ruled so insane he's put in an asylum. He seduces the head nurse, who's hot, but not in a slutty-fake-titted way, and she helps him escape so he can fulfill his dream of becoming a sex-positive therapist specializing in cunnilingus."

Now another sort of couple—a couple composed of at least one person who isn't a Drooling Fanatic—would have probably dropped Kip Winger as a thematic element at this point and proceeded to the evening's intended highlight: essentially comic sexual toil.

But my wife's reverie demanded a response. I reminded her that I was the one in the marriage who had spoken to Kip way back in 1989, when he was at the height of his powers, grand-jetéing his way through "Seventeen" and scheduling his groupies in fifteen-minute intervals. As my wife had probably forgotten, and I was now going to remind her, I had been a *professional music critic* once who possessed Kip Winger's personal phone number and who, what's more, had *covered the Grammys*. Once this was on the table, it hardly seemed fair not to provide a full account. My wife was lightly snoring now.

"Very funny," I said.

In the end, we compromised. Rather than mocking each other's Drooling Fanaticism, we spent the next hour fleshing out the Kip Canon:

Kip Karenina

Kip has a dilemma. Does he bang the totally hot Russian peasant babe, or does he go fight in the totally killer war? In the end, Kip decides to bang the hot Russian peasant babe, *then* fight in the totally killer war.

Moby Kip

Kip decides to head to New York City, where he inadvertently ends up at a Moby show. Backstage, he asks Moby about a possible collaboration. Moby responds by biting Kip's leg off.

The Grapes of Kip

Kip journeys to California as a migrant heavy metal bassist, enduring the prejudice of rich studio owners. Then his record goes gold and he hires Pamela Anderson as a wet nurse.

To reiterate: we were stoned.

I should add that Kip Winger continues to be a source of marital tension because my wife, in classic DF fashion, is convinced Kip will eventually read this and be offended. "I don't want you fucking up any future encounters," she told me recently.

"So it's still on with Kip?" I said.

"It was never off," she said. "I'm serious, honey. Don't fuck this up for me. Kip still looks good."[15]

15. In fact, my wife recently informed me, in a manner simultaneously abashed and ragingly proud, that she actually was the cause of Kip Winger getting an erection during their VH1 sponsored tête-à-tête, meaning that they had the equivalent of, I guess you could say, "terrestrial, close-range phone sex" is what I'm getting at, though she didn't want this vital elaboration printed in my book, lest it adversely affect her future chances with Kip, and, when pressed on the topic, suggested that Kip might one day in our future, our possible near future—wait, let me try to remember how she put this— oh yes, here it is: "come pirouetting into our bedroom in his leather pants," and was therefore, at this point in our story, suggesting that she wanted Kip Winger in our sexual lives, as a third in our threesome, and what's more, with that established, she went on to mention, with a sort of casualness that drives us doubt-choked Jews crazy, that Kip's wife was supposedly "smoking hot" and a swinger to boot, which it seemed to me (as a doubt-choked Jew) was the moment when she was actually envisioning a threesome consisting of:

a. Kip Winger
b. His smoking hot wife
c. Not me

This conversation took place on the eve of this book's publication, and therefore robbed me of the honor of titling this interlude "How My Wife Gave Kip Winger a Boner" or perhaps, more poetically, "Kip Winger's Boner."

12

Burying the Dead with Ike Reilly

I first heard Ike Reilly in the late summer of 2001. My career was in free fall. I had a literary agent, but she hated my guts, and just to show her who was boss I stopped writing prose altogether. All I did in those days was crank tunes and poop out wretched poetry. The Fanatic itch was thick upon me. And so, when a friend mentioned that the Tufts University radio station needed community DJs, I signed right up. I was summer staff at WMFO, 91.5 FM (aka The Mofo), taking my shifts in the great yawning midweek hours when the listenership dipped to seventeen.[16]

WMFO was where I found Ike Reilly's debut, *Salesmen and Racists*. Reilly sounded like—well, what did he sound like? He sounded like Dylan, if Dylan had been Irish instead of Jewish and never left the Midwest and grown up listening to the Clash rather than Woody

---

16. My show, *The Tip*, was part of the growing Drooling Fanatic empire I had established two years earlier, when I began distributing "a quarterly e-zine" of the same name. *The Tip* 1.0 consisted of a mawkish sermon on the virtues of socialism, followed by ten CD recommendations. Technically, *The Tip* was not a magazine. Technically, it was spam.

Guthrie. He sounded like Lou Reed and Gil Scott-Heron fucking each other, then fucking the Pogues.

It was inevitable that I would introduce The Close to Ike Reilly, because The Close kept a close eye on my fetishes. I had met him down South, at one of those literary conferences where midlist authors go to feel like rock stars. He had arrived with a trunk full of literary magazines where his stories had appeared, which he spent the week pressing upon us, popping up out of nowhere, yammering in urgent Jerseyese, his mouth very *close* to our ears. He fixated on me, having decided that I was the big brother he'd never had, a delusion that both flattered and alarmed me, as did the revelation that he lived around the corner from me in Somerville. Nonetheless, The Close and I became friends, in part because I felt a moral obligation to rescue him from his staggeringly banal taste in music, by which I mean the many hours he spent trying to get me to listen to "these killer bootlegs of Dave Matthews in Atlanta." One dose of Ike Reilly and I heard no more.

Soon, our phone conversations consisted of little more than Ike lyrics. The Close would say, "Well, if I go down in a plane I'll go to hell, but I'll leave all my shit to my friends in a will." And I'd respond, "You can have my Crown Vic and you can have my debt, you can have my weakness and my regret." And he'd say, "A beautiful girl once said to me, some men'll rob you with poetry and stay to watch you while you sleep and kiss your ears and make you weep." And I'd respond, "She's all whacked out, she don't back down, I threw my back out whacking that ass now." And he'd say, "Drink to the party, drink to the host, fuck this party, let's hit the coast." And we'd agree that we needed to hit the coast, ideally in a Crown Vic, with Ike and a staggering drug stash.

I knew that The Close would find his way to an Ike Reilly show, but I was out of town on the weekend in question. The Close appeared on my doorstep that Monday with an envelope of photos. "This is me with Ike," he said. "This is my girl with Ike. This is Ike looking at my girl's titties."

"Wait," I said. "You *met* Ike Reilly?"

"Hell yeah I met Ike. We showed up three hours before the show and drank with him. He drinks Red Stripe. He jumped off the stage and danced with my girl at the end of the show. Oh hey, I got something for you." He presented me with a small promotional poster. "That's signed," The Close said. "I had Ike sign that for you. Do we got any cigarettes or what?"

He was enjoying himself immensely, in particular the fact that I was infuriated. After all, I prided myself on being a "mature" Fanatic now, the kind who (generally) resisted overt Drooling. But The Close had an entirely different conception of Fanaticism. He weaseled what access he could, then flaunted it shamelessly. As I watched him flip through his photos, a horrible thought seized me: what if the little mooch was right?

I'm going to skip all the begging that led Ike Reilly to allow me to visit his home north of Chicago. It reflects poorly on my begging skill set. I will mention something fairly obvious: in the five years since *Salesmen and Racists*, Ike's career hadn't exactly exploded. "Why do you want to come see me?" he said, when I spoke to him on the phone. "I'm not a rock star. I got four kids. Seriously, you're going to be disappointed."

On the Road Again

Why did I invite The Close to come along? I had two reasons:

1. I was terrified to go alone and envisioned The Close as an ideal co-stalker in the sense that he lacks the capacity to feel shame.

2. If things took a turn for the worse, The Close could show Ike photos of his girl's titties, which he stored on his phone.

The potential snag lay in our record as road buddies; we had threatened to murder each other many times. The worst of our mis-adventures was a seven-hundred-mile trek across the South under-taken on the evening after the 2004 presidential election, the highlight of which was *not* listening to The Close urinate into a Gatorade bottle in the backseat, as you might expect, but listening to him ogle a group of prepubescent Mennonite girls at a McDonald's outside Roanoke. "*Mmmm-mmmm* virgins," The Close murmured, as the girls jittered in their bonnets. "Virgins taste good."

The mood inside our car was pure homicide. About all we could agree on as the black rain beat down was Ike. We had the stereo cranked so loud the crickets in the dark fields were swayed back in terrified silence.

A week before our flight to Chicago, The Close called to announce that his mother had died. To say he was estranged from her under-stated the situation. She had left her husband and three kids for another man. The Close had bragged to me once that he had spit on her when she appeared at the memorial service for his father.

Nonetheless, I told him I was sorry and I absolutely understood and we could still cancel his plane reservation.

"What are you talking about?" he said.

"The funeral," I said. "The arrangements."

"It's not a problem," The Close said.

"What do you mean it's not a problem?" I immediately launched into a big speech about how he had to try to forgive his mother and honor her death and how if he didn't he'd be hounded by Furies like Orestes and eventually need to be purified with pig blood.

"Hey, pally," he said impatiently, "this is Ike Reilly we're talking about."

And what could I say to that? Can you force people to feel what they need to feel? Can you force them to grieve? You cannot.

Dead on Arrival

Ike lived an hour north of Chicago, in Libertyville, the town where
he'd grown up. On the phone, he described his house as a "log cabin."
This made sense to us, because his lyrics suggested a working-class
hero, full of contempt for the swells. Thus our confusion as we pulled
into the Reilly homestead at nine in the evening—the "log cabin" was
actually a lodge, vast, exquisitely gabled, with numerous wings. The
driveway was the size of an indoor track.

"Where the fuck are the logs?" The Close said.

Ike wandered out to his driveway. He had striking blue eyes and a
nose Picasso would have adored, but his manner was that of a chippy
bantamweight, the sort of guy who had spent much of his life beating
up bigger guys.

The Close and I stood there staring at his lodge while trying not to
stare. Ike coughed uncertainly. Finally, he sighed and led us upstairs
to his studio, which looked very much like a ski chalet and included a
full bar. He introduced the Craiger, a burly Australian who served as
his driver/tour manager. Nobody quite knew what to do. Was this like
a journalism thing? Was I supposed to interview Ike? I pulled out a
notebook.

"No notebooks," Ike said.

"Remember me?" The Close said.

Ike squinted.

"Sure you do," The Close said. "Your Cambridge show, like, four
months ago. We bought you Red Stripes."

"Oh yeah," Ike said. "The guy from Jersey."

"That's right," The Close said. "Jersey. You danced with my girl."

This exhausted our small talk. We began chugging vodka tonics, in
the hope things would become less awkward. Eventually, Ike played us
a demo of his new record. The more we praised the songs, the more he
scowled. "It must be kind of hard to listen to your own music," I said.

Ike wheeled around and glared at me. I'd tripped some kind of silent Drooling Fanatic alarm. "Hey, you think this matters to me? You think I base my self-esteem on this shit? It's like I told you, this isn't who I am. I don't even know what you guys are doing out here." The room plunged into silence. "I'm supposed to feel like some big deal because I wrote 'Commie Drives a Nova'?" Ike sneered. "Please. How pathetic is that?"

I wanted to shout back that it did happen to be a big deal, that I'd watched "Commie" transform confirmed depressives into howling ecstatics and what's more that Ike was the only songwriter on earth who spoke the common language of punk and hip-hop and blues and Celtic music, the roiling rhyming bluster of motherfucking America. But Ike was still glaring, waiting for me to say the dumb thing that would justify giving us the boot. The Craiger dropped his big meaty fists onto the bar and awaited orders.

Sweeney Arrives

Just then, a large, red-faced human burst into the room. He was roaring drunk and eager to announce that his wife of many years, a beautiful woman, a woman he probably still loved, wanted a divorce. This was Sweeney. Sweeney and Ike had been pals since boyhood and their wives were best friends and Sweeney was thrilled to meet us because he was Ike's "number one fan on earth" and had many secrets to reveal about Ike such as that his real name was Michael but mostly he wanted to go out and *Get More Fucked Up.* "Let's get laid!" Sweeney roared. "I'm a free man, practically! Who's with me?"

It was nearly midnight on a Wednesday, but Ike wasn't going to leave Sweeney hanging and we were along for the ride because Sweeney had decided we were from *Rolling Stone* and were going to make Ike famous. We settled in at a bar downtown, where Sweeney held forth on a variety of subjects, such as the fact that, as a boy, he sat on the lap of Libertyville's most famous native, Marlon Brando.

"How did that go?" The Close asked.

"Great!" Sweeney bellowed. "He fisted me."

We stumbled through an alley to a second bar. At two a.m., Sweeney suggested we repair to his basement for alcohol poisoning. "I've got Tombstone Pizza! Who's in?" The Close set his head down on the bar and closed his eyes.

The Close Gives Me a Pep Talk

"Ike hates you," The Close observed the next morning.

It was nearly eleven. I had been up for hours already, fretting.

"Thanks," I said.

"I mean it; the guy really hates you. That shit you pulled with, like, psychoanalyzing him. Why are you always doing that?" The Close belched. He lay on his bed in our room at the Days Inn, wearing the kind of elaborate mid-length underwear you see on Sears man-nequins. "I thought he was going to punch you in the face. How does it feel to know that my friend Ikeal,[17] who I'm out here visiting as a *favor* to you, who obviously wants to get to know me, this guy now wants to punch you in the face?"

"I wasn't psychoanalyzing him."

"Your problem," The Close said, "is that you're a Hebrew. Moral instruction is embedded in your DNA. This mentality is the result of being a desert people. Deprivation and excessive nerves activate the prophetic impulse." The Close got up to piss, then burrowed back under the covers.

"You can explain all this to Ike over lunch," I said.

"There's not going to be any lunch, pally." He shook his head. "Talking to you is like talking to a dog."

Within a minute, he was asleep.

---

17. By The Close's formulation: *Ike + Michael = Ikeal.*

How to Score a Major Label Record Deal, Buy the House of Your Dreams, and Fail Spectacularly Without Really Trying

Ike did not blow me off. On the contrary, he showed up freshly showered, having just run ten miles. This struck me as something close to miraculous, given that he had consumed his own weight in alcohol a few hours earlier. But this was how Ike conducted business. His life amounted to an ongoing struggle between high ambition and low behavior. Years ago he'd refused a track scholarship in order to play rugby. He graduated college with a degree in political science and theology, then blew off law school to take a job as a bellhop at a Chicago hotel, where, if his songs are to be believed, he supplemented his income by serving as the unofficial concierge of drug sales.

His musical career had followed the same twisting path. He played with a series of bands throughout his twenties, including the Eisenhowers (this explained the nickname Ike), but dropped out of the music scene to support his family. He and his wife, Kara Dean, would eventually have four kids. In his mid-thirties, Ike began recording songs with a band of local guys, more or less on a lark. He sent a demo of this material to an acquaintance in L.A. Through a series of events too far-fetched to detail—but which Ike nonetheless detailed, in a series of digressions marked by radical shifts in tone, subject matter, chronology, and pronouns—this disc made its way to Mike Simpson, one half of the Dust Brothers. A few months later, Universal offered an ungodly sum for the record that would become *Salesmen and Racists*.

At this point, Ike did what any self-respecting American would: he bought a house far more expensive than he could afford. In his case, Log Haven, the elegant hunting lodge he'd visited as a kid and dreamed about ever since. It was approximately twenty times as large as the shitbox in which he and his family had been living. When he took his kids by to see the spread, they stared in confusion. His eldest asked him, "Are you going to be the doorman?"

Salesmen and Racists remains one of the greatest rock and roll albums ever released, and one of the least heard—which goes a long way toward explaining the chip on Ike's shoulder. In his mind, the label made at least two major mistakes. First, they chose as the lead single a song that opens with the lines "Last night I didn't make you come/Last night you didn't fake me out"—delightful lines to be sure, but not for commercial radio. Second, they sent Ike out on the road with John Mayer, which is something like asking Iggy Pop to open for Jackson Browne.

As petulant as Ike can sound about all this, it's fueled his creativity. He's released five raucously elegant records since *Salesmen,* all on a small indie label, and built a cult following. The commercial failure of his debut has become an inside joke among his bandmates, one of whom had a bunch of T-shirts printed up when Ike moved into Log Haven. They read: BIGGEST HOUSE, FEWEST RECORDS SOLD.

The Terror and the Drugs

After lunch, I went to pick up The Close. He had drawn the shades and lay in the darkness, looking pallid and frankly despondent. I wanted to ask if he was all right, if the aftershock of his mother's death had finally caught up with him, but I knew better. So we headed back to the studio, where Ike and his producer Manny hoped to lay down a demo for a new song. The following colloquy ensued:

> **Ike:** Hey. Did you sleep well?
> **Close:** Yes, I did.
> **Ike:** You know, I've got all sorts of pills.
> **Close:** Yeah, if you would like to give me some. My girl and I take them with wine.

Ike: So do I.

Close: Oh very good. You and I, we're the same. So I'll take any Oxycontin you've got.

Ike: I've got Oxycodeine. I've got—should I get them going now?

Close: No, I don't want one now.

Ike ducked out and returned a minute later. He pulled a handful of red and white pills out of his pocket, which he began cataloguing for The Close. The Close repeated that he wasn't in the mood for any pills. Then they both took a pill. Now it was time to record a new song.

Ike had told me about the song at lunch. He'd sung me the chorus, too: "Let's fight the war on the terror and the drugs." I didn't get it— had Cheney's people gotten to him? Ike picked up a battered acoustic guitar, played a blues shuffle, and began singing:

I need a girl, because I always need a girl,
Because I'm weak and I'm lonely in love

The song carried on in this manner for several verses. Then Ike's voice, which is most often a keening tenor, dropped to a whisper:

I dreamed that my children could not catch their breath
They were falling off buildings straight down to their death
Try as I could, I could not catch them
Before they landed and cracked open their heads

Out of their heads came laughter and lies
And frozen light and dark lullabies
I saw their sweet mother mixing their ashes and blood
But I didn't see no terror and I didn't see no drugs

At which point he roared into the chorus, and by which time I was roaring too (though softly), because the true purpose of that chorus had been revealed. It was a sly parable about the artificial wars cooked up by political admen, and how they obscure our true fears—the terror of losing those we love. This was classic Ike Reilly, a composition bristling with moral outrage but loyal to the needs of the pub crowds.

I had just watched my hero record a new song. *Boy,* I thought, *that wasn't so hard.* In fact, Ike spent the next six hours playing the same song, trying to settle on the right key (A to B to B-flat) and the right lyrics, which he had not bothered to write down and therefore kept tinkering with or forgetting or both. There was also the tempo, the phrasing, the best way to segue out of the bridge, and how to arrange the song for a full band. It was beginning to dawn on me how many decisions a musician had to make, which made the job seem—even in this most generative phrase—depressingly similar to writing.

Except that Ike would get a demo out of these sessions, which he could then give to his mates so as to effectuate that loud, collective feeling of *rocking,* to be transmitted (eventually) to a room full of sweaty fans, some of them young women whose beautiful tits would bounce up and down as Ike sang about the terror and the drugs and whose throats would produce lovely shrieks. This was not how writing worked.

The most charming aspect of watching Ike record a song was the constant intervention of his kids. His eldest son Shane called with a report from his soccer game. "How many did you score?" Ike shouted. "Against *them*? They suck. Yeah, well they *used* to suck." A bit later, we heard a loud scraping from outside. This was his ten-year-old, Kevin, tearing down the driveway on a new and spectacularly dangerous variety of skateboard. "Hey, Dad, check this out!" Ike stared at the boy. He clearly wanted to be down there watching his kid possibly crack his skull open, rather than recording a song about how frightened he was that his kids might crack their skulls open.

Then his oldest daughter, Hannah, appeared. She was a junior in high school, blond, beautiful, a star long-distance runner like her pop. Ike said that she might be visiting Boston to scout schools and The Close, who had mentioned that he taught at Boston University perhaps a hundred times by now, immediately got very close to her. "All right," he said, "the first thing is I'll give you a full tour. Then you can sit in on my class. Then we'll get you set up with the track coach. I'll call him when I get back."

"You can do that?" Hannah said. "You know him?"

The Close waved his hand like a magician.

"She's going to need a scholarship," Ike said.

"Not a problem, pally," Close said. "You just get in touch with me and I'll take care of everything."

The Wild One

Ike hadn't forgotten that we were Drooling Fanatics. But our presence in the studio had softened his basic contempt for us, so he took us to his favorite sushi place and we got shit-faced on sake. This made us all sentimental. Ike decided we needed to see a few of the local sights: the old frame house where he'd grown up, the alley garage where he and his pals came to get loaded, Brando's place. "There were times when I hated this town," he told us. "It was crawling out of me. That's why I identified with Brando. Terry Malloy. The Wild Ones. The group of guys I ran around with, that's who we wanted to be. I still lie to myself about where I am."

It occurred to me, as we cruised along the darkened shoreline of Minear Lake, that this was the central allure of rock and roll: the creation of a personal mythology. Rock and roll allowed people to lie about themselves, and to be sanctified for the extravagance of their fictions. This was how a mama's boy from Tupelo became our gyrating Jesus, how a nasally Jew from Hibbing, Minnesota, reinvented himself as a hipster messiah. Rock had enabled Ike Reilly to buy Gatsby's mansion and still shout the savage truths of punk rock.

We drove around for another hour. It was like touring the Stations of the Cross for a proud sinner. This is where Ike punched a guy through a storefront window. This is where Ike dangled his pal over the highway. At home he allowed us into the main living quarters, with its mighty beamed ceilings. The living room had been converted into a basketball court with a regulation-size hoop for his boys, over which a giant poster of Dylan kept watch. We met his lovely wife, who faithfully recounted Ike's domestic misbehaviors (Ike blasts the TV with a shotgun, Ike burns her wicker furniture in the backyard, etc.).

The night wore on. New drinks slid down our throats. Ike prowled from one room to the next and we stumbled after. We'd awoken his need to be perceived as something more than an aging rocker trapped in his hometown. Outside, the depraved winds of January howled. The moon hung like an ice chip. Ike played us song after song, the unreleased shit, the heavy shit. He rang our ears with incandescence and would not let us sleep.

The Close Mythology

And weren't we, as Drooling Fanatics, thrilled? I certainly was. But The Close had descended into a funk. He pulled me aside and insisted we leave.

"Are you crazy? Ike's playing us the unreleased shit!"

"I gotta get out of here," he snapped.

We drove back to the hotel in silence, and I knew what it was really about because, for all our teasing, I had come to love The Close, and he was an orphan now, whether or not he chose to admit that to himself. His mother was gone, he'd refused to make his peace with her, to forgive her transgressions, and so, by the dependable math of

Catholic guilt—and The Close, like Ike, was nothing if not a Catholic—he was now carrying her body on his conscience.

I thought about the afternoon, five years ago, when The Close's phone had rung and his voice had gone eerily flat. "How did you get this number?" he said, over and over. Then he hung up.

"Who was *that*?" I asked.

"My mother," The Close said. "The whore."

It was like staring into a part of him I'd never seen before. Because The Close had always portrayed himself as a comic figure, a profane braggart who enjoyed discussing the size of his cock and the sexual damage it might inflict on his lovers. I'd always laughed at this trash talk, but now it was seeming much less funny, more like the revenge he sought for his mother's betrayal.

The Close had been her firstborn, after all, and loved by her with unusual fervor. He had loved her too, as a child does, which is to say helplessly. He was a sensitive kid, melancholy, the sort who needs a mama. But she'd split, and he'd turned to his father, a paragon of male virtue. The Close spent his life trying to live up to that paragon, often to the point of caricature. I'd seen pictures of him in his early twenties, when he was a semiprofessional bodybuilder, a 'roid monkey down in Myrtle Beach, greasing his delts and posing in banana sacks. This was all part of the act.

But it didn't last. Depression walloped him into the waiting arms of literature. He left central Jersey behind and shipped off to grad school and found in words, in the turbulent rhythms of Gerard Manley Hopkins especially, a new passion. How did one explain this to a family of blue-collar Italians? *Hey guys, I'm in love with a repressed homosexual Jesuit priest poet. No, it's not like that. Really.*

Even before literature, though, he'd found music. His life was like mine, like Erin's, like the lives of all Drooling Fanatics, a struggle to reach the feelings forbidden within the confines of our families. He'd measured that life not in coffee spoons but in rock stars—Springsteen, Axl Rose, and now Ike, men who affirmed for him the rescuing power of personal mythology. This was why he'd insisted we split: it had been too painful for him to see Ike in such a needy state.

He'd never admit to any of this, of course. That was part of his confounding charm. But I knew he was hurting, somewhere beneath the bullshit. Just before sleep, I asked The Close if he was doing all right.

There was a lengthy pause.

"I feel like Ikeal got very close to The Close today," he said, in his loud Jersey voice. "He had a Close encounter. And as you could see, he did not want me to leave. He gave me drugs. He gave me songs. He damn near gave me his daughter."

"I meant more on an emotional level," I said.

"I think it's accurate to say that she's in love with me," The Close announced. "She's a girl of great heart and she recognizes another great heart."

We Are Only Here in Moments

Was Ike Reilly sorry to see us go? I still can't decide.

I know only that we were ready to go, having put undue pressure on the tenuous bond that exists between the Drooling Fanatic and his or her beloved. It wasn't that Ike had let us down. On the contrary, we left Libertyville more convinced than ever of his genius. It was what lived beneath his genius that spooked us, the immense doubt. We want, more than anything, to preserve our mythologies.

We sloshed south toward O'Hare under clouds the color of old nickels. Our rental smelled of chemical despair. The Close drove with the casual belligerence of his native state. I wanted to be able to do something for him. I knew he'd make himself pay later for this trip and this made me feel very tender toward him, very responsible. Only I didn't know what to do. Men can so rarely talk with any degree of honesty.

So I let Ike rescue us, as he had so many times before. *We are only here in moments,* he sang. And later, from another song, *Today we buried our mother/We laid the poor woman to rest/Everyone got a new suit/And my sister wore an ivory dress.* And The Close—poor Close!— who so loved his mother that he could only hate her, smiled and sang along.

Top Ten Covers of All Time

I hope it's good and clear by now that I have no business rendering critical judgments of pop music. There is one area, however, where I lay claim to being an expert: cover songs. I attribute this not just to my ongoing effort to convince every musician I've ever met to cover the song "No Scrubs" by TLC, but to the fact that in 2003 my pal Tim and I launched a series called Cover 2 Cover. Writers read their favorite writers, bands played their favorite covers, people got drunk, Tim flirted incessantly, and I got to be the DJ. This required me to compile a library of five hundred covers, from which I now happily skim the cream:

1. "Gin and Juice" by Snoop Dogg by the Gourds

Turning nasty hip-hop ditties into earnest pop ballads has become an indie trope. The Gourds tear it a new asshole. They render an almost tuneless Snoop song as a gorgeously textured bluegrass epic.

2. "I Just Wanna See His Face" by the Rolling Stones by the Blind Boys of Alabama

The original, a muzzy jam session tucked away behind "Ventilator Blues" on *Exile on Main Street*, finds new life as a gospel classic. Black folks ripping off the Stones—that's called *karma*.

3. "Mother" by Glenn Danzig by Matt the Electrician

So Erin and I walk into this club and there's this dude thrashing on an itty bitty stringed thing (half banjo, half ukulele) and growling gorgeously. "Omigod," I yell, "this is, like, the greatest song I've ever heard!"

"Honey," Erin says patiently. "This is a Danzig cover."

Fine. My judgment stands.

4. "Straight to Hell" by the Clash by Phil Cody

With apologies to Lily Allen, nobody comes close to Cody. He reaches into the guts of the song and produces a soaring elegy of disenfranchisement.

5. "This Is Not a Love Song" by PiL by Nouvelle Vague

What a joy to hear the screechy original revived as a voluptuous bossa nova. Johnny Lydon and his rotten teeth are no doubt horrified. Good.

6. "Voodoo Child (Slight Return)" by Jimi Hendrix by Angelique Kidjo

Covering Hendrix is a cottage industry. Kidjo creates an Afro space jam worthy of Fela Kuti. (Honorable mention to Bootsy Collins, who slips the scorcher "If 6 Was 9" a sex Quaalude.)

7. "Takin' It to the Streets" by the Doobie Brothers by Harry Manx and Kevin Breit

Every time I listen to this sublime instrumental I forgive Michael McDonald all over again.

8. "Istanbul (Not Constantinople)" by the Four Lads by They Might Be Giants

Because this is the whole point of a cover: you pay tribute to the source material while transcending it. What was a tepid swing tune explodes into divine weirdness via amphetamines and klezmer.

9. "How Am I Different" by Aimee Mann by Bettye LaVette and "Take It to the Limit" by the Eagles by Etta James

Or, in these two cases, lovely pop songs become soul classics. LaVette rips through the sadness and confusion of romantic abuse and produces an intoxicating rage. Etta takes the Eagles to church and baptizes their coke spoons in holy water.

10. "S.O.S." by ABBA by the Meat Purveyors and "She Drives Me Crazy" by Fine Young Cannibals by Dolly Parton

And here's the lovely thing I've discovered, which is that if you listen to enough killer covers—Dolly's sly hoedown, the Meat Purveyors' heartsick harmonizing—the very notion of genre starts to fall away, instruments, arrangements, none of it matters, all that matters is the song as a union of melody and rhythm, an expression of the universal language that is (in our moments of deepest need) a form of spiritual rescue, amen.

Why in God's Name Am I Managing a Band? The Boris McCutcheon Story

In the spring of 2003 I went to a Mardi Gras party at the Somerville VFW Hall. These guys started playing. They sounded like a Confederate marching band set loose inside a New Orleans brothel. There were, by my count, only four musicians on the bandstand, but that seemed impossible given the clamor. The drummer kept capping his runs with a sharp clack on the rim of his kit and the result was a delirious urge to bump butts with the person next to you. The hall was sweltering, but the lead singer wore a Sherpa hat with the earflaps down. He had chubby cheeks and a slightly stunned expression. Strangest of all were his lyrics, which he delivered in a drawl of indeterminate origin.

> *Why can't the whores (clack) blow the dandelions?*
> *Why do the girls (clack) always pass me by?*
> *I was hurt in an unusual way*

It made no sense. Except that the melody was a thing of such unbridled goofiness that this final line, serving as a refrain, began to infect the crowd, awakening in each of us the comic potential of our own self-pity, the conviction that we'd suffered some unprecedented romantic injury which our friends and family were simply dying to inspect. And thus whistles, shrieks, and hoots of "hurt!" started to rain down in the style of a tent revival. I spent the next half hour dashing around the party, trying to find someone who knew the band.

"That's Boris," this girl said.

"Boris?" I said. "Boris what?"

She shrugged. "He's from the Cape, I think."

Someone pointed me to a pretty blonde, the band's manager, and I nearly tackled her. She happily supplied the singer's full name (Boris McCutcheon) and a copy of the album his band was about to release, *When We Were Big*. I've tried many times to describe *WWWB* in the years since. I usually settle on something like "Sam Cooke fronting The Band." This makes no sense, because Cooke had a silky tenor whereas Boris sings in a sandpaper baritone. The point of comparison has more to do with the commanding quality of each man's voice, the immediate sense upon hearing them that you had better stop what you're doing and listen. I'm also trying to get across that Boris is a soul singer, someone who draws on the traditions of gospel and R&B, even if the arrangements place him in the vast hinterlands of Americana. It's like he's found some hidden trove from the Smithsonian Folkways series and run them through a Motown filter.

Boris Days

And did I likewise, on that first night, assail the members of the band and buy them drinks and invite them back to my apartment to party until it was too late for Boris to drive back to the Cape so that he and his dog Pappy eventually passed out on a spare futon in my front room? I think so. Or maybe that was another night. There were a lot of them back then, because Boris and his backing trio—they would later be called the Salt Licks, but for now had no name—were soon playing the smaller clubs around Boston and I was coming out to every show, with a variety of women (Erin being one) who quickly discerned that I was more interested in the band than in them.

There was, to take another example, the night the band and I constructed a chocolate Jesus in homage to the Tom Waits song. And the night Bones, the bass player, spent in panicked consultation with Poison Control because his dog Chopper had eaten one of my ant traps. Dogs were a constant in the Boris days, big friendly mutts who munched on poison or got sprayed by skunks or snarled at one another, doing their bit to add to the chaos.

The essential chaos, the human nexus of it, was Boris himself, Boris of the broken trucks and disconnected phones, of the lost capos, of the songs scrawled feverishly on the backs of receipts smeared with motor oil and stashed in the tackle box with his harmonicas. He spoke in a soft growl and dressed like a mestizo farmer; he had no fixed address. One week he was crashing on a farm in Woods Hole, the next he was with Bones down on the Cape. His pattern of employment was equally erratic. My friend Mitch likes to tell the story of seeing Boris play a Brookline pub and bumping into him the next morning, fixing a sprinkler on the Boston Common. He'd taken a post as an irrigation manager for the city, though he departed some weeks later, after dropping his key ring down a sewer grate, a blunder requiring the closure of a major road and the deployment of numerous city employees along with a giant scooper. He would later memorialize this episode in the song "17 Scoops."

This was how Boris operated. The turmoil of his life invoked the refuge of music, where he found, if not quietude, at least an ordered universe. He knew which notes would produce beauty, how to arrange them, which details to include, the optimal tempo, how the song sounded in his head, and how to make it sound that way in the world—an act of scrupulous translation that is the essential vocation of a musician. In this pursuit, he could not have been more disciplined.

And so for me there was really no choice but to see him play every chance I got, for the pleasure and inspiration, and because I knew this wasn't going to last long, Boris was going to rocket to fame or explode into ruin or both. His band knew it too. But Boris was a genius, and genius establishes its own centrifugal force. They put up with a lot of shit on his behalf, cursed him regularly, and remained ravenous for his attention.

The band had just formed when I first saw them. Over the next year they grew into the sort of outfit you always hope is going to appear in your neighborhood bar but never does. They were fast, loud, tight, completely in synch and somehow, at the same time, able to project the aura of drunken pals just playing for beer. Some nights the lineup included a lanky tuba player, much favored by the ladies for his disheveled Teutonic beauty. Or a stray mandolin player. Where did these folks come from? Nobody knew. They just appeared, vomited whole from the Borisphere.

In early 2004, the band booked its first foreign tour—of Holland. I was sure this meant the band had arrived. I volunteered to ferry some equipment to the airport for Boris, but when I arrived at the apartment where he was crashing, nothing was packed. Gear and clothing lay strewn in a cyclonic tableau. Black electrical cord, miles of the stuff, snaked down hallways, over banisters, under sofas. Boris himself was red-eyed and muttering. He needed to burn two hundred CDs before sundown, to sell in Holland. It was four in the afternoon. It never occurred to me that this state of affairs might suggest a fundamental ambivalence in Boris.

The Green Wish

It would take another year for me to start to see things clearly, and I spent as much of that year as I could with Boris and his mates. I was doing other things too, such as teaching and writing and falling in love with Erin and breaking up with her. She loved Boris, too, and accepted that there were going to be some nights, many nights, actually, when I found it necessary to party with him and the boys until dawn.

That spring, Boris invited a bunch of us down to Naushon, a small, undeveloped island just off the southern coast of Massachusetts. His mom held the august title of the island's Livery Stable Manager and Chief Shepherdess, and her home had become Boris's crash pad of last resort. Naushon was like something out of a brochure for Ireland: low stone fences, green hills dotted with sheep, hidden coves. There were thirty-five homes on the island and no roads. Boris took us on a winding hike to a house on the remote western end. He had something to show us.

We found the place by late afternoon. All the doors were locked. Austin, the guitar player, spotted a screened window and we hoisted him up and he shimmied through and crashed to the floor. The air inside was thick with mothballs. Boris led us to a tiny parlor containing his surprise: a miniature keyboard that appeared to have been played last during the Spanish-American War.

"What is that?" I said. "A harpsichord?"

Boris seated himself and began pumping the thick pedals under the keyboard.

"Pump organ," Bones murmured.

Boris set his hands on the keyboard. For a second, we heard only the clack of the yellowed keys and the soft thud of the pedal beneath. Then notes began trickling out of the pipes. None of us recognized the tune; it was something he made up on the spot I suspect, a boogie-woogie by way of Aaron Copland. He closed his eyes and his face tilted slightly up, then his voice joined in, majestically, and the particulars of the song seemed absorbed into something larger, an ancient feeling like jubilation.

This was life with Boris. Music lay at the center of everything. He had led us astray and risked the injury of his lead guitarist, but now, as the sun set over Buzzards Bay and golden light flooded the room and dust motes made wild circles around his head, we stood behind him swaying and nobody said anything for a long time.

Later there was dinner and booze and pot. Boris busted out his guitar and played a few new songs. He was writing all the time, between gigs and travel and the jobs taken and not quite kept. We all waited, in those months, for what he would write next, our desire being not a greed for proximity or ownership, but for particular forms of beauty and what they might reveal about ourselves.

I remember the night, a few months later at my place, when Boris pulled out his mandolin. (I didn't even know he owned one.) We were sitting on the green couch in my sunroom. His bandmates were scattered around the place, passed out amid the homemade bongs and stinking curs and puddles of chocolate goo. My future wife, a figure of possibly masochistic patience, lay curled in the bedroom.

Our throats were raw and our souls were wired; they always were in those days. Boris began plucking at the strings absently, coaxing himself toward sleep. But the notes resolved into something more solid, a chugging minor-key progression. Then Boris began to sing in his burred baritone and I felt the holy shiver. The song was built around a single line, chanted like an incantation: *The green wish is here.* Such a phrase! I figured he'd nicked it from Isaiah. The song ended and Boris grinned shyly. The mandolin lay in his lap like a polished stone.

"'The green wish,'" I said. "What's that?"

"Spring," he said softly.

Chicken Man

And then there was the time Boris asked me to help him write some lyrics. See, he had this one swampy blues song called "Chicken Man" that he sometimes played at the end of shows. But it needed a couple more verses, which I supplied within twenty minutes of his request. This meant we were coauthors if you wanted to get technical about it, which I certainly did.

A few months later, at a concert I'd organized for Boris called (I kid you not) "Rock and Roll Will Save Your Life," the band started playing "Chicken Man" and Boris stepped to the mic and mumbled, "Hey, I can't remember the words to this one. Is Steve Almond here? Let's get Steve up here to sing this one."

Wasn't this what I'd wanted all along, what every Drooling Fanatic longs for, the chance to be born again? Here it was! The crowd let out a whoop. Only I was scared to death, in the same way I'd been scared as a kid whenever I wanted something too much. I would forget the words or hit a flat note or, most likely, I'd get up there and do my best and people would applaud my Drooling exuberance, then it would be over and Boris would take back the mic and everyone would look at me with the minor pity of this recognition.

Or worse, maybe they wouldn't. For a second, I saw myself seizing the microphone with snarling brio. *What a voice!* everyone would say. *We'd thought he was a writer. But really, he's a rock star!* This would explain why, for instance, I was so miserable, why, though I was putting books into the world and occasionally reading from them in public, I still hated myself and hated what I did, the stupid precious intent of all my decisions. Maybe I *would* lose myself in the song. Maybe I *would* produce the beautiful roar I suspected lay hidden inside me, and thereby confirm my true calling—and then where would I be? I'd be Joaquin Phoenix, basically, minus any possible hope of success.

And so I stood there in a queer paralysis of desire and dread. My friends turned to me. Someone tugged at my shirt. It was like one of those scenes from the movies where time slows down and everyone's face gets really big. Boris was staring at me, too. But I couldn't speak.

Instead, I watched my hand rise up and begin to flutter, as if to brush away his kind offer. The Chicken Man had made his debut at last.

Oddly, this realization did not crush me. On the contrary, it came as a relief. I was now free to focus my fervor on promoting Boris. I started booking gigs for him, and sending ardent letters on his behalf to my "contacts" in the music business.

It was this last stunt that provoked a letter from his actual manager, Jeannie. She wanted to know whether I would be "stepping in as his manager/promoter/assistant." Her note was incredibly gracious, given the circumstances. She'd devoted two years of her life to Boris. Hell, she'd sold her house to fund the making of *When We Were Big*. But by late 2004, she was fed up. So were his bandmates. Much as they loved and revered Boris, they were tired of working for free. Boris himself was involved with a woman who had moved to New Mexico and was pressing him to head west.

Thus, in addition to ad hoc manager, I now assumed the role of band therapist. I listened to everyone bitch about everyone else and made sympathetic noises and told them that yes, they had every right to be upset, absolutely, but they also needed to be patient and forgiving of each other. My folks were both psychiatrists, so this rap came easy to me.

I might have been less determined had Erin not headed west herself, for grad school. But she was gone by September. Once again, I was a would-be lothario adrift in my thirties, an absurd figure in baggy sweaters and dumb facial hair. I knew adulthood lay waiting with its domestic props and duties, and this made me cling all the more dearly to the turbulent brotherhood of the band. Hanging out with them had become (I can now see) an idealized version of my youth, in which the brothers in question didn't pound each other into hamburger, but had drug-addled sleepovers and shared secret nicknames and made beautiful music together. I'd been allowed to become a part of that, and I sure as shit wasn't going to let it fall apart.

In Which It Falls Apart

Because of course it does.

The half-life of any rock band boils down to a brutal formula: Ambition multiplied by Luck, divided by the Tolerance of Loved Ones. Boris told himself he wanted to be famous. He certainly wanted the conveniences of fame: money, respect, someone to drive you around places. But he resented the promotional labors involved, the necessary humiliations.

His patter, for instance, was almost impressively incoherent and his mood sometimes ornery. One night, at an Irish pub in Newton, he introduced the guys in his band but neglected to mention his name.

"Who are *you*?" someone yelled.

"I'm Boris," he snapped back. "Who the *fuck* are you?"

As the final months played out, I began to feel less like an advocate and more like an enabler. Boris told me he needed money to print more copies of *When We Were Big* and I loaned him the dough. Then he needed more money, because he wanted to record another album, in New Mexico, and needed to fly Austin and his drummer Jeff out there, so I organized a Halloween fund-raiser at the Somerville VFW. I was back in the club promotion business, and just as bad at it as ever.

After the party, I stood with Boris in my bedroom and handed him the take, a wad of twenties fat as an onion. He slashed figures down on a piece of paper and detailed what he was going to do with the money, as if I truly were his manager now, as if we were mapping out some grand strategy. I could see right then that the era we had shared was over, the money would evaporate and his mates would move on and maybe a record would get made, and maybe it wouldn't, but the dream, which had something to do with fame but more to do with the redemption every fan seeks in offering his or her unconditional love, that was over, too, because my patience had finally run out.

"You figure it out," I said, and I left him there, piling stacks of dirty bills on my bed.

A Pony Ride to the Other Side

This story is supposed to end with both of us retreating obediently into domestic lives, never to be heard from again. And it's true that we did marry our long-suffering girlfriends, more or less in unison, though I believe Boris managed to get through the ceremony before knocking his bride up. It's also true that Boris left Boston. He moved to New Mexico, to a tiny pueblo at eight thousand feet. His occasional e-mails spoke of solar panels, an outhouse, a second child. So I figured that might be that, I'd never see the palooka again. Then, in April of 2008, he called to tell me he was coming back east for a show in Woods Hole.

"Have you told any of the old crew?" I said.

"Huh," he said. "You think I should?"

I could feel the old promotional juices start to flow again. I could make some phone calls, get a caravan organized. But I didn't have an afternoon. I had a pregnant wife and what the pediatricians call a "busy" toddler and not quite enough money. In the end, I drove down with my friend Mitch.

We found Boris at the Community Hall in Woods Hole, a high-ceilinged building that appeared to be floating on Buzzards Bay. He was finishing up a sound check with his band for the night: his loyal bassist Bones and a sweet-natured guitarist named Brett. Boris looked a bit heavier. A stripe of whiskers ran down his chin. Bones was busy transcribing the chords for one of Boris's new songs, which he was expected to perform in an hour. They filled an entire page. "'Proud Mary' has three fucking chords," he said to Boris. "Why can't you write a song like that?"

At ten minutes to showtime, the crowd numbered a dozen. Both

Mitch and I tried not to notice all the empty seats. Was this what it had come to? Boris couldn't even draw folks in his hometown? But we had misread the locals. They showed up late: old-time hippies, families with fleeced children, teenagers hopped up on candy bars and hormones. Someone who brought a salt lick from her farm and set it onstage. We had underestimated Boris, too. His trio sounded lovely, even without a drummer and a proper rehearsal. His new songs killed. He told a story about getting into a fight with his wife and taking off driving and spotting an old Mexican man offering pony rides in an empty parking lot. Then he launched into a country stomper that sounded as happy-go-lucky as a song can, until you took note of the words:

> I've got a Special Forces wife
> with a tongue like a bowie knife
> Can I have a fucking pony ride?
> I want a pony ride to the other side
> I want a pony ride to change my rotten perspective

And what was crazy about this song was that I, too, had just gotten into a fight with my wife, who did not have a tongue like a bowie knife but who did, like Boris's wife, have a second child in her belly, and who had likewise grown tired of my selfish artistic needs as they related to my husbanding duties, and I too felt as guilt-ridden and enraged as Boris, as knee-deep in diapers and debt, as in need of a pony ride. The song rang my heart like a bell.

The band kept playing and the songs did their mysterious human work. At half past nine, Boris announced that the last ferry was leaving for Naushon in a few minutes. Most of the crowd needed to catch that ferry, but nobody moved. Boris clamped a capo onto his guitar and murmured, "Okay then, we'll play one more." It was a lullaby he'd written for his daughter, a waltz, and it made everyone in that hall a little drunk. How strange life seemed to us then, how petty in its demands, everyone always needing to get somewhere. Outside, the moon was rising. The stars were arranging themselves above the sea with great patience. Boris stood in a black western shirt and played his old guitar. His voice never sounded so beautiful.

Interlude:
A Frank Discussion of My Mancrush on Bob Schneider

I have to start here, because if I don't my wife will eventually read this and say something like, "Aren't you going to mention your massive mancrush?" to which I'll respond, "Shut up! I so totally *don't* have a crush on Bob!" to which she'll respond, "Then why do you talk to the poster of him on your wall?" to which I'll respond, "I admire him as a musician. Why do you have to make it into something *dirty*?" Then I'll slam the door in her face and throw myself down on the bed and stare up at my Bob poster, the one with him looking all yummy and stubbled, and wail, "Don't listen to her, Bob! She's just jealous!"

Nobody wants that.

So let me start by noting that every Fanatic is entitled to at least one homoerotic crush, which means, for gay Fanatics, a heteroerotic crush, the point being that there's some musician out there whose talents and manner and physical presence completely jam our normal sexual circuitry.

This all started back in 2002 when I went to see Bob play for the first time. I expected ragged versions of the catchy stuff from his new album, *Lonelyland*. But Bob utterly destroyed the template. He thrashed his prettiest ditties into punk screamers. He segued from bluegrass to cabaret to drugged-out dub and made everything seem effortless. At one point—this was during a mambo—Bob swung his guitar behind his back and sped the time signature. His bandmates followed suit, including the keyboard player, who hoisted a very heavy-seeming electric piano onto the back of his neck. The song became a sweet torrent—and nobody missed a note.

When it was time for an encore, his guitarist ripped off a Frampton talk-box solo circa 1978, which somehow led to a four-part harmony of "Mercedes Benz" only with guitar riff lifted from "Sweet Home Alabama," though at a certain indefinable point you realized they were playing "(You Make Me Feel Like) A Natural Woman" and none of this, not one note, came off as glib. On the contrary, these covers were entirely devout. Bob was saying to the crowd: *Here's where my music comes from. And here. And here.*

Though in fact, Bob spoke very little to the crowd. He didn't jump around. He didn't *need* to jump around. He had his chops to recommend him and his physical magnetism, which was that of a leading man—Tom Hanks, say, if you drained off the goofiness and retained only the required assets: the jaw, the penetrating gaze, the husky baritone. He knew there was a row of hotties camped beneath him in push-up bras and fellatio dreams. He could hear the frat boys hooting. He recognized the desires and pleasures of the crowd as a condition of his being. I'd never seen such poise.

I had no idea who I was dealing with at that point. I didn't know Bob had spent a decade fronting the two most raucous party bands in Austin's hallowed party band tradition, that he appeared to know every song ever written, and to have written half of them himself, that he was (in short) not just a hunky troubadour but a variety of musical savant, the most charismatic and prolific songwriter of our proximate generation, the most fearless and versatile, and certainly the filthiest.

Man Meet Mancrush

A passel of label honchos appeared at Bob's next Boston show. The place was mobbed and Bob had shaved for the occasion. During an instrumental break, he walked offstage and wandered over to the VIPs and I remember thinking, as I watched this brief and devastating charm offensive, *How can you not make this guy a superstar? He's destroying this club before your eyes. He writes hits in his sleep. He's dating Sandra Bullock—and he's better looking than Sandra Bullock.*

That's not what happened, obviously. The next time I saw Bob, he was hidden behind a thick beard and he played a suite of songs so sad they could only have been the result of dashed love, meaning he and Sandra were splitsville. (*Us Weekly* had the deets.) *Lonelyland* had yielded one minor radio hit. The six months he'd spent in the studio trying to produce a commercial follow-up had nearly driven him mad.

How did I know all this? Because it was my job as a Drooling Fanatic to acquire such details. I also did some minor stalking. This is how I discovered, a few shows later, that Bob had gotten married and had a son. I spotted him and his wife pushing a stroller down Commonwealth Avenue several hours before his gig. I startled them by handing Bob a copy of one of my books, which I'd inscribed *just in case I saw him.*

So now he was married. That was cool. It's not like I wanted to marry the guy. What I wanted, as I explained to his publicist, was to spend a week on the road with him. This would allow me to document him writing songs about the colorful folk he encountered and jamming with his killer band and (last but not least) poolside escapades, meaning, in the greater interests of rock and roll, sunbathing in the nude together and doing bumps of coke off the greased pubic bones of teenage virgins. His publicist suggested a brief interview at his home as perhaps more realistic.

On the morning of my interview, I woke with my gut in knots. I was in the Houston airport, waiting for a flight to Austin. The sky kept spitting threads of lightning and then, I shit you not, hail started to fall, making an eerie *ping-sizzle* on the roof of the terminal. My head was stuffed full of bad outcomes. The airport would close due to apocalyptic weather. Or no, better, I'd be electrocuted at 37,000 feet. Such are the dark visions that plague a Drooling Fanatic on the brink of meeting his mancrush.

Bob lived west of town, in a development whose ambience suggested a suburban game preserve. I imagined a ranch, acres of rolling pine, a hayloft where we could go to be alone. But Bob's house was small and nondescript. There were no cars in sight. A bouquet of white daisies was rotting beside the walkway. The lantern hanging above the front door was full of dead leaves. I rang the doorbell. Dogs started barking. After several uneasy minutes, two large canines came bounding toward me. Bob appeared behind them, pale and dazed. "I forgot you were coming by," he said.

How Not to Woo Your Mancrush

Inside, I began sputtering in the precise manner I'd told myself not to sputter. I couldn't stop myself, because I'd grown up in the shadow of two handsome brothers and developed the common American misconception that physical beauty makes people smarter and nobler, and because I was seeing Bob at his ugliest and he was still better looking than Christ.

The living room was scattered with toys and the computer on the kitchen counter was flashing photos of his son. It suddenly seemed important that I inform Bob I had a wife and child, too, a life beyond the borderline creepy feelings that had brought me here.

> **Me:** This must be your son. Very cute. What's his name?
> **Bob:** Luke.
> **Me:** Good name. Good gospel. How old is he?
> **Bob:** Three.
> **Me:** I have a daughter who's one.

Bob: Cool.

Me: So are you planning on having any more?

(Long Pause)

Bob: No.

Me: Stopping at one, huh? Yeah, my wife and I are thinking of having another, not really trying yet, but also not really not trying, if you know what I mean. Ha-ha-ha.

(Very Long Pause)

Bob: My wife and I separated two years ago.

Now many things began to add up rather quickly. Such as why there was no sign of his wife or child. Such as why Bob had been asleep at ten a.m. Such as why the premises exuded dishevelment. (What kind of woman allows a pile of white daisies to rot in her front yard?) A more observant person—a writer, for example—might have figured this out. I stood, blinking.

"I'm gonna go get dressed," Bob said.

I was ready to apologize and leave. It was obvious he didn't want to be talking to me. And in a weird way, I wasn't sure I wanted to be talking to him either. I'd forgotten the sheer dread that is a central ingredient of hero worship. But then Bob reappeared and said, "You wanna grab some breakfast tacos?" and my heart thumped out a Y-E-S.

The joint was called Jim Bob's B-B-Q. It was across the street from a mall. In fact, it was surrounded by malls. This was the new Texas prairie; Lowe's had run off the longhorn. Inside, the TV was tuned to Fox News. Bob ordered a Diet Coke and an egg and potato breakfast taco. The cashier set a Styrofoam cup on the counter for his soda, then handed me my change, which *I immediately tossed into Bob's cup.*

How to explain this action?

Near as I can figure, I was so determined to seem like the kind of guy who tipped, to impress Bob with my casual generosity toward the service industry, that I somehow managed to put aside the fact I had seen the cashier put the cup on the counter and, ergo, it was obviously *not* a tip jar.

Things were not going well.

Die Young, Hope Somebody Notices

Back at his house, I asked him if it was true that he'd learned how to play guitar at age three. He nodded. His father, a professional opera singer, had made him learn so he could perform at the parties his parents threw. "People ask me all the time, 'How should I get my kid involved in music?' And I'm like, 'Well, be completely unavailable to them unless they play music.'" He laughed, but not happily.

Bob eventually came to the University of Texas at El Paso, to study art. I had hoped to bond with him over our El Paso connection, but he dropped out of UTEP after a few semesters and relocated to Austin, just as I was arriving in town.

His musical evolution over the next decade provides a convenient survey of unfortunate nineties genres. He did white boy rap/funk (Joe Rockhead). He did roots/jam music (Ugly Americans). He did party rock (the Scabs). "I knew exactly what the plan was when I moved to Austin," Bob said. "I was going to become a huge rock star and die at twenty-seven. So I got into bands and drank very heavily and did as many drugs as I could. I just never got successful enough to die properly. Nobody would have cared."

Yes they would have! I wanted to scream. But I was afraid Bob would take it the wrong way so I asked if I could use his bathroom. This was a mistake. The moment I closed the door I melted down. I knew on one level that I was a writer with a semiplausible reason for being in Bob Schneider's bathroom. But on another level—a far more emotionally convincing level, frankly—I couldn't stop thinking: *Ohmigod! I'm in Bob Schneider's bathroom! That's totally, like, his toilet! He sits right here! He sure does read a lot of art books! He uses really cool soap!* Then I came out of the bathroom and Bob was sitting there, looking exactly like himself. I had to take a few deep breaths to calm myself.

She Don't Mind the Cum, G

I had been in Bob's presence for a full hour without doing something stupid, so I decided to ask the question I had been waiting to ask since I arrived: would he go steady with me?

No, that wasn't it.

I stared at my notebook and tried to decipher my handwriting.

"Why aren't you more famous?" I said.

"Oh, I've always been a massive star in my own head," Bob said. "The weird thing for me is when I look out into the audience and I'm not playing for more people and I think to myself—and it seems extremely arrogant—but I think, 'At this point, with this band and this set, we should be playing giant stadiums.' I've always wanted the external world to line up with that world in my head, but at the same time I've never been willing to do the things necessary to achieve that."

In fact, this was a big part of what made Bob Schneider so incredibly crushworthy to me. With his looks and his chops, he could become the next Jack Johnson without breaking a sweat. But he has absolutely refused to clean up his act. I submit as Exhibit A his recent composition "Hocaine." It is about dating a crack whore.

> If you got the Humvee, she don't mind the cum, G . . .
> If you got the thick bills, she's got the sick dick skills . . .
> If you got the magic powder, she'll let you give her a golden shower

I don't suppose it helps to note that this is the *least offensive* portion of this song. Nor that it is generally performed to a jaunty piano riff appropriated from "This Land Is Your Land." But here's the thing: while a certain part of me recognizes how offensive I should find this song, another part of me finds it incredibly liberating. And because I myself have done best as a writer when I focus on the abundant depravities of our species, it inspires me to encounter a guy who refuses to censor himself just to get ahead. When Bob told me that he wanted to call his new album *Fuck All You Motherfuckers* I had to physically restrain myself from climbing into his lap.

A Kingdom of One

It was time, as they say in Reality TV, to take this bromance to the next level. Or at least to Bob's studio. He led me out past a small pool with leaves in it, to a shack inside of which were more instruments than I've ever seen in one place: guitars, banjos, mandolins, a baritone ukulele, what was either a xylophone or a marimba (Bob wasn't sure), an ancient Wurlitzer that made a mysterious buzzing noise, a small drum kit in the center of the room, a baby grand piano. The room's lone chair was surrounded by banks of synthesizers, mixing boards, and computer monitors. It looked like where a starship captain would sit. And Bob was, in a sense, a starship captain. Using this equipment, he could record, edit, and mix songs all by himself.

The studio doubled as the HQ of his record label Shockorama, on which he's released a dozen records in the past decade. In fact, he'd meant to release *Fuck All You Motherfuckers* months ago, but it was still sitting on his hard drive, along with hundreds of other unreleased songs. (The rumor was that Bob sometimes wrote a song per day.)

It will sound hokey, but I honestly felt like I was standing in a holy place. I had 559 Bob songs in my iTunes library. I had listened to his music for entire days at a time and thought about him, in some capacity, every day for the past five years. I recognized the chance that we would run off together was extremely low, but I also believed—and I think Drooling Fanatics cannot help themselves in this regard—that I understood Bob in a way nobody else on earth did, that we were soulmates and though he didn't know this yet he had a secret message to impart. This is perhaps the most annoying aspect of Fanaticism, from the musician's point of view. They owe us nothing beyond their songs, but we keep hounding them for more.

"How do you do it?" I asked. "How do you write so many totally ass-kicking songs?"

Bob replied that it wasn't really him, it was his unconscious, he was just plugging into it, like you might plug a fork into an outlet. "There's this weird thing that happens with songwriting," he went on. "When you first start doing it you're just doing your best with whatever comes into your head, but after a while you get this idea about what's good or bad and you start doing this approximation of what you think you should be doing and the only solution I've come up with is just to keep my standards low."

Yes, I wanted to cry out, *that's it! You, Bob Schneider, have just identified the fundamental crisis (and resolution) of the creative process. Might I now briefly stroke your big beefy man hand?*

But Bob wasn't finished. He said, more to himself than to me, "Sometimes I wonder if I wasn't me, would I like what I do? Like, a few days ago I did a show and right before I went on, I started thinking, 'I suck, I truly suck, and I kind of got lucky on a few songs, but they're kind of worn and I'll never write anything good again and I'm washed up and what's the point and why am I doing this and if I had any other options, if I hadn't painted myself into a corner, I'd take them.'" He shook his head. "I don't have a life. I really don't. I spend as much time as I can with my kid, but the rest of the time I work, period. You see that pool out there? I've swam in that pool fifteen times in five years. You and me hanging out like this? I never do this. When you came and rang my doorbell this morning, I was like, 'Nobody comes to my house, nobody rings my doorbell. Ever. They just don't. Maybe it's the exterminator.'"

After a moment, Bob continued, "In every relationship I get into it's like, 'Why do you spend so much time working? I feel lonely. I want to interact with you.' And the reason I do what I do is that I feel I have to do it to justify breathing; I don't have the sense of self-worth that allows me to not do it. People come up to me at shows and they'll say, 'Your music means so much to me.' And I always try to be nice to them and appreciative, but I'm not doing it for them. I'm doing it so I can save myself from drowning." He added, quite softly, "We live in a society that puts a high premium on success and I learned, mainly through my dad, that salvation would come through success, and I carried that into my adult life and it's a total lie."

I was hit hard by all of this, not just the sudden darkening of Bob's mood, but the acute solitude he described. It seemed to me that his ambition had become a kind of Oedipal curse, a way of vanquishing his father while also clinging to the sorrow of his childhood. Music put him in the spotlight and, at the same time, it had become the instrument of his exile. He had pushed his wife away. He had no real friends. His studio was a monument to his musical invention, but it was also a fortress, so crowded with the tools of his trade that there was room for no one but himself.

Wave Good-bye to That Man You Love

And what could I say to any of this? It was the old story about being careful what you wish for. I wanted to comfort Bob somehow, to confess my crush in a way that would return to him some of the joy he'd given me. And then on the other hand I wanted to get the hell out of there and hug my wife and baby daughter. It's a strange feeling, to worship and pity someone simultaneously.

Later that night, more or less by accident, I would attend a raucous dinner party and wind up sitting across from a woman in the local music scene. I told her I was in town to interview Bob Schneider. She fixed me with a quizzical look. "How did it go?" she shouted.

"Kind of awkward," I shouted back.

"It always is these days. I don't know what's happened to him. When he was with Sandra they used to come out all time . . ." I couldn't hear the rest of what she said but I could tell by the look on her face that she was being wistful, recalling happier days, and it made me wish that I'd never come to Austin at all, that I'd behaved like a reasonable fan, and not invaded the desolation in which his art continues to bloom.

14

How Dave Grohl Taught Me to Stop Whining and, Against Every Known Impulse in My Body, Embrace Happiness

I was asking Jimmy at the valet stand where I might find some decent food, because we were on Sunset Boulevard, where all the tourist joints smell like frat. "There's an In-N-Out down there," Jimmy said.

"How far?" I said. "Walking distance?"

Jimmy looked at me like I'd asked to lick one of his tattoos. "Whatsamatta," he said, "you don't got a car?"

A drunk guy came stumbling out of the hotel. He had a sideways Mohawk and a T-shirt reading GET YOUR OWN, BITCH. His female companion was the color of the cheese mix you add to Kraft macaroni. Something in his manner, the belligerent public inebriation, I guess, suggested he might be a rock star.

"Hey," I said to Jimmy, "was that guy a rock star?"

Jimmy made a sound like he was going to spit. "None of these people are rock stars. They're rich Eurotrash who come here so they can *act* like rock stars. The Strip is all poseurs now. Not like it used to be. Man, you don't even wanna know how crazy that shit used to get."

Jimmy was right. I didn't really want to know how crazy that shit used to get. But he proceeded to tell me anyway, because the Sunset Strip is one of those self-consciously famous locales—L.A. is lousy with them—where the natives feel a civic compulsion to recite the prevailing mythology.

I was only chatting with Jimmy because the rock star I was supposed to be interviewing for *SPIN* magazine—Dave Grohl, former Nirvana drummer and Foo Fighters front man—had blown me off. It was Labor Day, 2007, and I'd been in Los Angeles for forty-eight hours and had yet to spend a single minute with Grohl. Instead I'd spent those hours fielding increasingly frantic calls from my editor, who wanted to know why I had yet to spend a single minute with Dave Grohl.

I was so far from knowing the answer to this question that it had become an indeterminate philosophical inquiry. There was an entire circuitry of power and influence crackling around me, a network of publicists and managers and agents and editors, all of whom were yelling at one another on cell phones about access and contingencies and deadlines and all of whom sounded helpless. My life had become a Beckett play, as adapted for the stage by Chuck Klosterman.

My editor was taking it the hardest. It was his ass in the sling. To make up for lost time, he wanted me to fly to Las Vegas to join the Foos for the MTV Music Awards, a plan that sounded glamorous until you realized that it would almost certainly involve me sitting in a hotel room, listening to my editor stroke out on the phone.

"Oh hey," Jimmy said. "There's a California Pizza Kitchen down on Holloway."

My cell phone rang and it was not my editor. It was someone named Eliot, who worked for a music publicity firm employed by the Foo Fighters. Eliot had flown from New York to Los Angeles for the express purpose of making sure I got access to Dave Grohl. The Foo Fighters, in other words, had just paid thousands of dollars to lobby themselves on my behalf. "Let's make this happen, buddy," Eliot said.

I turned off my cell phone and fled Sunset on foot. The sidewalks were littered with scuffed photos of young women eager to degrade themselves and flyers of bands who had already failed but didn't know it yet. Down I plunged, through the lavender smogcrust, which registered as a corroding warmth in the throat. On Santa Monica, I passed an open-air club called RAGE where young men in underpants danced on raised boxes. They looked smooth beyond all feats of epilation, as if they had been flayed. The patio bars were packed for Labor Day. Billboard faces loomed over the avenue, vast and pale, like planets of narcissism. My cell phone buzzed. I had six new messages.

Not Famous, Not Almost Famous

If you're wondering what it's really like to write a cover story about a rock star for a national music magazine, this is what it is like. You spend a lot of time talking to people like Jimmy at the valet stand and staggering through hotel lobbies on the verge of nervous collapse.

As to why I took the assignment, this was a complicated question. I'd long since sworn off rock criticism. At the same time, some crucial part of me wanted to see what it was like to be a Big Famous Rock Star with No Integrity, and how such a life might differ from other sorts of lives, such as my own. Whatever cultural sophistication we might aim at, no matter how many Obscure Rockers with Integrity we might visit, the Drooling Fanatic remains an essentially covetous personality. Also, *SPIN* was offering more money than I had earned in ten years as a short story writer.

Foo headquarters was in the San Fernando Valley, which meant numerous trips over the dirty yellow mountains that divide the hip part of L.A. (mansions, movie studios, boutiques) from the unhip part (strip malls, porn sets, ethnic worker bees). The first time I arrived at the Foo compound, some asshole in a black Beemer pulled up behind me and laid on his horn, then burned rubber into the parking lot. That was the closest I would come to interacting with Dave Grohl for the next two days.

Instead, I was left to skulk accusingly while the Foos got their photos taken by Japanese magazines and huddled with managers and rehearsed, in private, for the MTV gig. I wasn't even the only reporter on the premises. A guy from *GQ*, who looked about seventeen, was getting major face time with Dave. I was eventually reduced to eavesdropping on the band's inane conversations during photo sessions, a practice I suspect produces 50 percent of the quotes printed in *SPIN*.

Why couldn't I just set up a time to interview Dave Grohl? Because there was a protocol, one that operated on two levels. The first was practical. Grohl was a rock star who ran his own multimillion-dollar-yet-still-impressively-disorganized corporation. He had no fixed schedule and eighty people required his attention at all times. The second level was psychological and largely subconscious. It was predicated on the fact that a reporter was an interloper, a nonfamous person, an envoy, in fact, from the larger world of nonfamous people. The idea that a nonfamous person would make a demand on the time of a famous person is inherently offensive to the keepers of celebrity.[18]

Journalists are dependably loyal to this protocol, because their professional stature depends on access. When that access is promised then suddenly denied in irrational ways, when you are basically standing around in a strange place far from home with an unctuous publicist as your only ally, it makes you angry, but more than that it makes you very very needy. And so when you finally get to talk to the

---

18. For a micro version of this dynamic, consider the last live show you attended. Did the band members begin at the time advertised? Of course not. They sat in the green-room and bitched about the deli platter. This delay not only sold lots of overpriced beer for the club, but served as a potent reminder of the power structure. You might have acted annoyed, but deep down you were relieved. The band's negligence affirmed your status.

rock star (or movie star or politician or athlete) in question it's like they've rescued you from a terrible nightmare, which is the nightmare of your own helplessness and your unfamousness and your accession to the shitheadedness of fame, and by your affiliation with them you are temporarily elevated into the world of the semidivine. This is one of the reasons celebrity profiles are so fawning: because they manage to capture a spirit of slavish gratitude that is the result of weeks (sometimes months) of hegemony and self-colonization.

I hope this helps explain why, the first time Dave Grohl spoke to me, approximately fifty-nine hours after we were first supposed to meet, six hours before my return flight to Boston, I was so instantly grateful, so starstruck, so possibly and confusingly in love, that I could only nod my head and fight back tears. Grohl didn't just say hello. He walked up in plain view of his posse and smiled at me and said, "Hey man, you're always so mellow. I love this guy. We've got to get some time to hang out. Can you hang out tonight?"—an outburst of such diabolical psychological brilliance that for a few moments I actually felt guilty. I was going to have to blow Grohl off to catch my flight. *Man, I'm sorry, Dave.*

But then I realized that this was how they got you, these famous people. They made you feel responsible for their burdens, then gave you the slip. So I said, "Could we talk right now?"

"Yeah," he said. "Sure man."

There was nowhere private we could go except the bathroom. This was how I wound up interviewing Dave Grohl in the crapper. I wasn't sure where to sit, but he dropped right onto the floor and I sat across from him, a bit closer to the toilet than I maybe would have liked. Here's the thing about Grohl, though. It didn't even matter. Because he was so completely the opposite of what I expected (i.e. egotistical, bratty) that he came off as *the least neurotic person I'd ever met.* Within five minutes, he had confided in me about his idyllic childhood, how he met and wooed his wife, the drug overdose that nearly killed his best friend, drummer Taylor Hawkins, how this trauma helped convince him to have a baby, and how much he adored his baby. Then he lit up a cigarette and offered me one. We'd just had celebrity profile sex.

Ghost in the Machine

A minute later, Grohl's manager knocked on the bathroom door and told him that the crew from Wal-Mart had arrived to shoot the official Wal-Mart promotional video for the new album. The Foo Fighters were very tight and very loud and Grohl himself sang in such a manner that the veins in his neck turned red and sort of vibrated. It was impressive.

Afterward, I stood in the lobby of Foo HQ, considering what would happen if I didn't get any more time with Grohl. And what I realized (depressingly) is that I already had enough material. It almost doesn't matter what you write when it comes to celebrity profiles. The only salient point is that you got access. So if you're wondering how much face time you need to write the cover story for *SPIN*, the answer is ten minutes. *Rolling Stone* is more exacting; you probably need twelve minutes.

As I was thinking this, Grohl strolled over and invited me to swing by his house. This, too, was a calculated move, because he knew that I had a baby daughter at home and he, too, was a new father; this would give us something over which to bond. So I followed him up to his mansion in the hills above Encino and interviewed him on the veranda and met his stunning wife and watched him goof around with his stunning daughter and change her diaper.

But here's the strange thing: while I recognized that Dave Grohl and I were engaged in a deeply contrived scene, staged expressly for PR purposes, hanging out with him made a deep impression on me. He was the first musician I'd met—hell, the first artist—who'd achieved stardom without turning his life into shit. Who, on the contrary, had maintained the tranquillity of his domestic life despite the pressures of fame. In fact, the reason he'd blown me off for the first two days of my visit was so he and his wife could interview nannies.

Grohl's equanimity struck me as even more remarkable given that he'd spent his early twenties backing Kurt Cobain, the modern archetype of self-destructive rock stardom. I assumed Grohl, having spent so many years in Cobain's shadow, would avoid talking about him. But I was wrong. As we sat out on the veranda, Grohl, apropos of nothing really, volunteered that he'd been watching a YouTube clip that morning, of Kurt's home movies. "He's hanging out with his family in a park," Grohl explained. "Sitting by this stream as these little girls run around, and it broke my heart because I knew when that was and I knew that he wasn't necessarily happy at the time." Grohl shook his head. Down below him, the L.A. sunset stood ready to flare. A few feet away, his beautiful toddler Violet Maye was circling a barbecue grill, murmuring to herself *hot hot*. "He couldn't fully experience the joy of life," Grohl said softly. "And I'm at that point now where I can."

Grohl looked dour for a moment. Then he looked over at Violet and scooped her up and suddenly I had a pretty good idea why Cobain's ghost had been sucking around. It had nothing to do with the burden of living up to his genius, or even his loss as a friend. It was the simple and horrifying fact that Cobain was, at the time of his death, the father of a girl almost exactly Violet's age.

The Myth of the Suffering Artist

So there I was talking to Dave Grohl, but what I was thinking about was my friend Lee, who wept the day after Kurt Cobain died and insisted that he was our generation's John Lennon. I hadn't said this to Lee at the time, or to any of the millions of other DFs voicing similar sentiments, but this struck me as dead wrong. Lennon wrote hundreds of songs, in a wide range of emotional and musical vernaculars, and became one of the most important political activists of his era before he was murdered. Cobain wrote in one genre, in two moods at most, and shot himself in the head while on heroin. He was instantly canonized for this act, which totally fucked over everyone in his life.

So what I was thinking about, really, was the Myth of the Suffering Artist, the obdurate notion that success should come at the expense of happiness. I was thinking about Boris and Nil Lara and Ike Reilly, guys who had twice the talent necessary to be stars, but who remained essentially neglected figures. And I was thinking about myself (as usual) and the ways in which I identified with these guys because of my own knack for greeting creative triumphs with self-punishment.

Bob Schneider had told me this story about touring with Dave Matthews and how charming Matthews was to everyone and how much this had made everyone want to help him. His point was that charm was the crucial ingredient to making it big. But I saw something more fundamental in Grohl. He struck me, above all, as an empathic guy, someone who had resolved his internal conflicts, the guilt and grievance that we use to bar ourselves from the kingdom of happiness. Maybe he wasn't Saint Kurt of the Wounded Heart,[19] or Mozart or Van Gogh or Rimbaud, but he was a genuine artist doing his best with his given portion of talent and being kind to the people around him.

Hokey as it may sound, the guy struck me as a role model just then. Because so often in my life I'd assumed that the only score that

---

19. Let me add for the record here—knowing it to be a mortal sin against Rock Critic Dogma—that I consider Dave Grohl a more talented musician than Kurt Cobain.

mattered was the one for artistic merit, and that I was almost duty-bound to screw up everything else on its behalf. That wasn't how I wanted to measure success anymore. I wanted to be a loving husband and father, a good friend, a conscientious citizen, someone whose life affirmed the compassion of his work. Maybe that meant that I'd never be anything but a midlist toiler. But why did I need to be anything more? Why did anyone?

Hell, wasn't the very concept of "fame" a modern pathology? For most of our history as a species, after all, fame didn't even exist. The only true celebrities were figures from mythology or religious stories. And there was no commercial barrier to creative expression. It was enough to be able to sing or tell a story or ride a horse with grace or make a beautiful shoe—these talents were recognized for the immediate pleasures they provided.

But somewhere along the line we'd convinced ourselves that acts of imagination only had value if strangers would pay for them, or if they won fancy prizes, or if critics decided they had merit, notions that had proved a boon to the Myth of the Suffering Artist. Because now, in addition to the anguish that arises from trafficking in unbearable feelings, artists had to worry about these vile forms of regard.

It was a fucking crock, and I wanted to tell Dave Grohl as much. But we were too deep into our own fame charade to turn back at this point. Grohl did his best to make it bearable. He remained friendly and self-deprecating, and even though his estate was at the top of a mountain and contained a tennis court and a waterfall, he made a joke about how the terra-cotta roof tiles reminded him of a Chi-Chi's franchise. When I mentioned that I'd be back in L.A. soon he asked why and I told him for a reading and he said, "Hey, I'll have to check that out."

We were standing in Dave Grohl's circular driveway, gazing down upon the Valley of the Non-Famous, unto which I would be descending momentarily. A gleaming turquoise Harley was parked beside a tiled fountain. I wanted to say, *Look man, you don't have to try so hard.* But it seemed important to Dave Grohl that he be the sort of rock star who would show up at a reading given by the reporter interviewing him, and it seemed wrong, given all he'd taught me, to dash his hopes.

List #6

I See Your Muffin and Raise You a Pirate: The Many Silly Names of Rock Star Spawn

Back when Erin first got pregnant we spent hours yakking about What to Name Baby. This is pro forma activity in the age of overdetermined parenting, as is giving your fetus a nickname. Ours became Peanut. There was a brief stretch during which we seriously considered making it legal, or at least enjoyed terrorizing the grandparents with this prospect.

Eventually our daughter was born and somewhere in the midst of this howling endeavor the gravity of the parental mission dawned on us. Yes, Peanut Almond exuded a certain snacky insouciance. But here was this actual person, very small, very frightened seeming. Giving her a gag name suddenly seemed just a tad indulgent. We settled on Josephine.

The fascinating thing about rock stardom is that it seems to impart the opposite lesson: that naming a child is an activity that should, above all, reflect the cheeky creative spirit of the parents in question. Had we been rock stars our child almost certainly *would* have been named Peanut Almond. Or Marzipan Almond. Or Chocolatta Joy Almond. And I know this because the roster of actual strange rock star child names is so expansive that they can only by catalogued by genera. (As a special added bonus, I've made up one name per genus.[20] Happy hunting!)

Genus: *Flat-Out-Bat-Shit-Crazy*

Audio Science (Shannyn Sossamon)
Speck Wildhorse (John Cougar Mellencamp)
Pirate (Jonathan Davis of Korn)
Zowie (David Bowie)
Rebop (Todd Rundgren)
Seven Sirius (Erykah Badu and André Benjamin)
Annarchy (Buzz Osborne of the Melvins)
Bamboo (Big Boi of OutKast)
Elmo (Curt Kirkwood of Meat Puppets)

Subgenus: *The Majestic Remix*

Messiah Ya'Majesty (T.I.)
O'Shun (Tamika Scott of Xscape)
Jhericurlicious (Rick James)
Jermajesty (Jermaine Jackson)
God'lss Love and Heaven Love'on (Lil' Mo)
Keypsiia Blue Daydreamer (Big Gipp of Goodie Mobb)

Genus: *Tragically Misguided Cutesiana*

Heavenly Hiraani Tiger Lily (Michael Hutchence of INXS)
Fifi Trixibell (Bob Geldof of Boomtown Rats)
Nutella Sphinx (Roger Waters of Pink Floyd)
Zuma Nesta Rock (Gwen Stefani and Gavin Rossdale)
Bluebell Madonna (Spice Girl Geri Halliwell)

---

20. My "source" on all of this is a consortium of Internet sites, meaning 75 percent of these names are probably total bullshit. Sorry.

Subgenus: *Pottery Barn Paint Swatch*

Saffron Sahara (Simon Le Bon of Duran Duran)
Sonora Rose (Alice Cooper)
Humboldt Green (Phil Lesh, Grateful Dead)
Blue Angel (The Edge)
Dandelion (Keith Richards)

Subgenus: *Inexplicable Feline*

Tiger Lily (Roger Taylor of Duran Duran)
Rufus Tiger (Roger Taylor of Queen)
Ocelot (Shannon Hoon of Blind Melon)
Calico (Alice Cooper)
Puma (Erykah Badu)

Subgenus: *Redneck Boutique*

Shooter (Waylon Jennings)
Gunner (Nikki Sixx)
Justice (John Cougar Mellencamp)
Steelin (Toby Keith)
Fordtuff (Alan Jackson)

Genus: *Pretentious Homage* (subgenus: *Musical*)

Devo (Maynard Keenan of Tool)
Django (Dave Stewart of the Eurythmics)
Jagger (Scott Stapp of Creed)
Jazz Domino (Joe Strummer)
Nina Simone Smith (LL Cool J)
Manilow (Clay Aiken)
Thelonious (Mitch Dorge of Crash Test Dummies)
Wolfgang (Eddie Van Halen)
Zeppelin (Jonathan Davis of Korn)

Hendrix Halen Michael Rhoades (Zakk Wylde of Black Label Society)

Subgenus: *Historical/Literary*

Galileo, Artemis (Alex James of Blur)
London Siddharta Halford (Sebastian Bach)
Raskullnikov (Slash)
Electra (Dave Mustaine of Megadeth)
Tamerlane (John Phillips of the Mamas and the Papas)

Genus: *Geography for $200*

Harlem (The Game)
Atlanta (John Taylor of Duran Duran)
Memphis (Bono)
Burkina Faso (KRS-One)
Island (Gregg Allman)
Egypt (Treach of Naughty by Nature)
China (Grace Slick of Jefferson Airplane)
Kenya (Quincy Jones)

Lifetime Achievement Award: *Frank Zappa*

Moon Unit and Dweezil get all the ink, but my faves are Diva Thin Muffin Pigeen and Ahmet Emuukha Rodan. When asked why he saddled his children with these names, Zappa famously replied, "Because I could."

That's *so* rock star.[21]

---

21. The phony names are Annarchy, Jhericurlicious, Nutella Sphinx, Humboldt Green, Ocelot, Fordtuff, Manilow, Raskullnikov, and Burkina Faso.

Dayna Kurtz Sings the World a Lullaby

You will have noticed by now an apparent gender bias in my Fanaticism. Nor can it have escaped your attention that I have some issues around attraction to men, who happen to outnumber women by a wide margin in the rock star category, anyway. But I'm going to suggest that the main reason my musical Dream Team is a sausage party is much simpler: I creep out female musicians.

I have certainly tried to inflict my Fanaticism on several, the most ignominious example being the night I showed up at a small club in Cambridge to see Shivaree and specifically that band's alluring lead singer, Ambrosia Parsley, whom I followed backstage and stared at in mute wonder until security was summoned. I have made repeated efforts to secure an interview with Neko Case, but I can never get past her publicity people, who seem to have a sixth sense when it comes to Drooling Fanatics posing as music journalists. And yes, it is true that I once spotted Patty Griffin down in Austin and pursued her on foot, but she lost me in a strip mall. (I'm pretty sure it was her.) There is no shortage of female artists I find Droolworthy—Beth Orton, Bettye LaVette, Nikka Costa—merely a shortage of female artists who will have anything to do with me.

The single exception (and she happens to be my favorite female artist of all, so good luck there) is Dayna Kurtz. We met five years ago on a Sunday night in winter. Dayna was playing a dumpy bar in Cambridge, the same bar where, two months later, I would read from my first book and not quite meet Erin. There were four people when I arrived. I waited for the late rush. There was no late rush. The late rush was me. The moment Dayna opened her mouth the room was filled, instantly, with a deep human trembling.

I knew this was going to happen because I'd been taking her new record, *Postcards from Downtown*, intravenously. The other four people in the bar were there for dinner. They talked over her songs at such a volume that she eventually asked them to please quiet down. They ignored her. Dayna had every right to stop. But she gave herself to those songs, fully and without embarrassment. She sounded like Billie Holiday and Leonard Cohen whispering into the same mic, and her melodies were swollen with the complicated joy of sorrow.

Afterward, I went up to apologize for the loudmouths. Dayna was tearing through a hamburger. She wanted a quick getaway and for this reason she allowed me to help lug her gear outside to the car. Only there was no car. We walked up one block, then another, then turned around. The situation slowly dawned on her. "Fuck," she said. "This is so fucked up." She began to weep.

It would emerge that Dayna had driven seventeen hours straight to reach this gig, from a festival where she played for seven hundred fans and had the opportunity to share a bottle of wine and a hot tub with the folk god Greg Brown, events that would have marked the zenith of her career to date. Instead, she now stood in the freezing cold on a Cambridge street corner, following the worst gig of her life, her car stolen, with a twitchy Fanatic—hi!—as her sole consolation.

I had some good news, though. Her car had not been stolen. It had been towed. I knew this because my car was towed on a weekly basis. So I drove Dayna to the impound lot, got her aimed back toward

Brooklyn, and drove home flush with small-time heroism. It hadn't occurred to me back then that the life of a musician could be so unglamorous. I had a lot to learn.

Candles, Roses, and Wine

I am still waiting for Dayna Kurtz to become a superstar. I was sure it was going to happen in 2004, when she released the record *Beautiful Yesterday*, which featured a duet with Norah Jones. But the only song of hers most Americans have heard is the version of "Twinkle, Twinkle, Little Star" in the television ads for Sheraton hotels.

The fortunate part of this unfortunate situation is that Dayna remains accessible to me. We've become friends of a sort over the years, which is to say she's read a couple of my books and I've listened to all of her albums five thousand times. In March of 2008, as she prepared to record a new album, she invited me up to her cabin to watch her work. The place was nestled in a valley on the western edge of Vermont, twenty miles from the nearest highway. I arrived in the late afternoon. The bales of hay looked as if Monet had painted them. The mountains were an iridescent green. Little tufts of cloud drifted across the fields. (These were lambs, it turned out.) Dayna appeared on the porch. She is a tall woman with wide-set eyes and a husky voice.

We took a walk through the local farmland. Dayna pointed out a barn where monks made artisanal cheese. The white birches shed elegant scrolls of bark. It was all quite Vermont. Dayna told me she did a lot of her brainstorming on these constitutionals, recording melodies and lyrics onto her iPod. She'd been hiking the area since she was a kid, back when the family cabin was a shack with no running water. It was still a pretty undeveloped area, but the cabin had been updated to "modern rustic" status. You could now listen to the brook babbling out back while lounging in the Jacuzzi.

Dinner was an Italian red sauce with country spareribs whose deliciousness was such that I would have eaten my own arm if covered in this sauce. Dayna had worked as a cook after graduating from UMass Amherst with a history degree. Her parents had hoped she might pursue academia or the law, but she was determined to be a folksinger.

This shouldn't have come as a complete shock—Dayna did teach herself to play piano at age three. Her early compositions, however, did not augur well. "My songs were *highly* confessional," she told me. "I had a lot to say and I said it a lot. The arrangements were self-consciously complex. The first song I wrote, at seventeen, was called 'Candles, Roses, and Wine.' I had another one called 'This Side of Eve.' I don't need to play them. You know exactly what I'm talking about."

Dayna eventually settled into a familiar folkie pattern: playing bars to support her coffeehouse gigs. Every few years, the music industry would go through one of its *time to sign chicks* phases and the A&R guys would show up full of golden promises. The president of the label would blow smoke up her dress. Then the proposed deal would fall through, because the marketing tools had no idea how to get her songs on the radio.

Dayna had started out as a Joni Mitchell devotee, but as she traveled the country, she became increasingly drawn to native musical forms. Her songbook soon ranged from orchestral waltzes to Appalachian nocturnes performed on banjo. There was also the problem of her looks. She was like a scary, grown-up version of Fiona Apple, not an emaciated waif willing to roll around on shag carpet in her underpants, but a sturdy Jewish girl from Jersey who schlepped her own gear.

As her thirties dawned, Dayna had yet to make a studio album. She was approaching what music professionals call an "unsignable age." Then a strange thing happened. *Postcards from Downtown*—recorded in the home studio of her drummer—exploded in Europe. Overnight, Dayna could fill a theater in Amsterdam or Barcelona or Berlin. In the

Netherlands, she was considered an alt-country artist. In Spain, she played festivals with PJ Harvey and Beck. In Germany, she headlined jazz clubs. She played the same songs in each country, the same arrangements. But each crowd recognized in them the expression of a distinct American musical tradition. And all of them were right.

Everybody Must Get Stoned (Again)

After dinner, Dayna led me downstairs to the room she was converting into a studio, on whose floor she'd been sleeping the past few nights. ("I'm trying to get my scent into the corners, you know?") In years past this situation might have posed temptations—the Drooling Fanatic finds nothing sexier than a musician in his or her native habitat. And we were, after all, miles from any seat of judgment. Thankfully, we both recently had married Drooling Fanatics of our own. We settled for getting baked out of our skulls. I'd brought Dayna a bag of something called "Black Widow" grown by a friend of mine who, not incidentally, is a competitive eater.

It was at this point, I believe, that the original plan—for Dayna to "work on the new album"—took a detour. The first part of this detour consisted of us babbling. I did my *Roving Petrol Mobs Are Going to Kidnap My Daughter* rap and my *America Will Die of Its Own Greed* rap, both of which my wife has heard so many times that she will actually ask me to recite one of them when she's having trouble sleeping. That somehow led to a conversation about which came first as a form of communication, words or music? I'd originally thought music, but then I'd heard a news report in which scientists managed to replicate the sounds produced by Neanderthal Man. Neanderthal Man, in turned out, sounded a lot like Mr. Roboto.

Dayna shook her head. "Lullabies," she said. "The first noise was some sort of primate humming to her baby. They've done studies and lullabies all over the world have the same arc; they all rock like a cradle."

"Yeah, but at what point did humans switch from getting something across to getting something out?"

"Drums," Dayna said. "Guys getting together to drum and chant."

"*Iron John* was right," I observed. "That's depressing."

It was around this time I began entreating Dayna to play me some new songs.

"I should warn you," she said, "I've been getting really into rockabilly lately."

"Rockabilly?" I said. "Really?" As much as I respected Dayna's musical explorations, I associated rockabilly with the Stray Cats, who played the same annoyingly jumpy song for the entire eighties. I hereby accept the collective animus of Rockabilly Nation, but we all have our taste and to me rockabilly has always exuded a swagger that feels monotonous within two minutes. It's the Fonzie of rock genres.

Dayna picked up her bass guitar and began playing a melody that was the aural equivalent of a chocolate cupcake. Her strum hand kept a clacking rhythm and her voice tilted up into a Hank Williams half-yodel on the choruses. By the time she was done, I was ready to pomade my hair.

Then, just for good measure, Dayna pulled out her new double-headed lap steel guitar and sang a crushingly sad version of the Replacements' "Here Comes a Regular." Listening to Dayna's voice was like a drug. It wasn't just her tone or her range or her power, which, if I knew anything about vocal technique, I could praise at length. No, it was something emotional. Her voice sounded like desperation hurled into the world with exquisite control.

The song ended and I set about trying to explain to Dayna how much her voice meant to me, how much, over the years, I'd needed her songs to plumb the dank morass of my own feelings, how without her music, without "Paterson," I suspected I'd still be alone, without my wife, without my blessed daughter, a lonely Fanatic grinding language into self-regard. I was getting choked up.

Then Dayna did something truly mean—she stuck a guitar in my hand. Like Boris, she had sensed in my desperate DF energy the longing to make music. Dayna attempted to teach me three chords that, she assured me, would allow me to play the entire Rolling Stones' catalogue. But my fingers were too runty and weak to hold the finger positions and any talent I had for muscle memory (none) had been eroded by the pot, so Dayna went to Plan B: an open tuning. This would allow me to flail at the strings without worrying about making chords.

I did this for a few minutes, while Dayna strummed a guitar of her own and filled the air with all sorts of sweet lies—*You've got a great ear! Listen to that! You're totally making music right now!*—all of which, by their insistent benevolence, served only to confirm my regret. It was time for bed.

But I had to ask one more question, because my heart was woozy with self-pity. The ensuing exchange should be read with the long, profound pauses of the late-night stoner implied.

Me: What's it feel like when you're performing?

DK: Being in the middle of an electrical storm.

Me: You see! That's exactly why I'd be happier as a musician.

DK: Most of the musicians I know aren't happy.

Me: They have to punish themselves for the ecstatic experience of playing music.

DK: All artists torture themselves—especially Jewish ones.

Me: Yeah, but you guys have so much more to torture yourselves *for*. You have these moments that are transcendent.

DK: There's not that many moments.

Me: Yeah, but there's *some*, that's my point.

DK: You have some transcendent moments when you're writing. You have to.

Me: No, I have moments where I stop hating myself briefly.

DK: You'd feel the same way if you were a musician. That's just you, honey.

Dayna meant no offense. On the contrary, this is how Jews show affection: the deadpan acknowledgment of one another's neuroses. She was a very maternal figure, really. It was obvious in how she treated me, and especially in her songs. "Bedtime," Dayna said.

She led me upstairs and turned on the Jacuzzi. "It'll help you get to sleep," she said. No musician wants a stoned Fanatic prowling her house at three a.m. Dayna padded downstairs to sleep on the floor of her studio, while I undressed and slipped into the Jacuzzi on the back deck. The river down below roared softly. The sky was a milky veil. I thought about a comment Dayna had made earlier. "The thing you have to understand," she said, "is that your relationship with music wouldn't be so deep or pure if you were a musician."

Dayna had given this matter plenty of thought. Hell, she'd married a Drooling Fanatic. Then again, maybe she was just pitying me. I thought of my hands struggling to form a G-chord on the neck of Dayna's guitar. I thought of all the times I'd taken up an instrument and waited for the magic to seize my body. I thought of all the musicians I'd drooled at over the years, and how happy I'd imagined they must be, and how sad so many of them seemed when I actually visited.

I had always fantasized that learning the language of music would grant me passage to a realm beyond sadness, that I'd find some sunny version of myself tucked away inside the current mess. But maybe I had it wrong. Maybe it was in music itself—the sounds as my body and heart received them—that the magic resided. Maybe my failure was some kind of subconscious effort to preserve the joy of being a Drooling Fanatic. I closed my eyes. I could hear Dayna singing, very slowly, very softly. *Here comes a regular, am I the only one who feels ashamed?* It took me a full minute to realize that I was the one singing; the words were coming out of me.

Outro

Drooling Fanaticism
in the Age of Actual Drooling

A few years ago my pal Tom Finkel called me up. "You know what's great?" he asked, not bothering with hello. "Listening to Bob Dylan with your baby daughter." I'd never heard Tom speak with such contentment. I could hear Dylan in the background. I imagined Tom lying on the couch, the kid curled on his chest. She would have been three months old.

I've thought about that phone call a lot recently. It connotes a certain fantasy: that Drooling Fanaticism and parenthood are not only reconcilable, but ideal dance partners. Who better to indoctrinate into the pleasures of song than your children?

It hasn't worked out quite that way in our household. Our two-year-old Josie does love music. But she does not now, nor has she ever, wanted anything to do with "my music." She's got her own music—and woe unto thee who fucks with her playlist. My wife learned this a few months ago when she walked into the child's room. "I want *Dino 5!*" Josie shrieked. *The Dino 5* is a dinosaur-themed children's hip-hop album. It is exactly as charming as this description implies.

"Oh, honey," my wife said, "not *The Dino 5* again."

Josie's face, her entire being, crumpled.

"She wasn't upset that I was saying no to her," Erin told me later. "It was that I'd insulted her music. It was like I'd just done the worst, most hurtful thing in the world. Oh, God." Erin was herself close to tears.

Now that Josie can reach the pink boom box we stupidly placed in her room, she will play the same album, sometimes the same song, up to twelve times in a row. It is for this reason that I know by heart the words to songs such as "Bouncin' Baby" by Justin Roberts:

Bouncin' baby bought a bag of blue jeans
Bouncin' baby bought a big ole bag . . .

Over which I have puzzled for entire weeks, as to what sort of baby would buy blue jeans in the first place, especially a bag of them, and what would make this baby prone to bounce and whether there's any correlation between infant elasticity and retail buying power. It is probably fair to say that fatherhood has exacerbated in me certain tendencies toward procrastination. I also know that if we don't get Josie's *Music Together* CD on within five seconds of entering the car, all hell will break loose, as it will if I try to slip on one of my albums. ("No! No papa music!")

All this has reinforced my belief that Drooling Fanaticism is an innate tendency, something that gets bred out of us as we grow older, like playing with our food. It is certainly true that when I find a song I love—Sam Roberts's "Detroit '67," say—my natural impulse is to play it twelve times in a row. The reason I don't is because I've learned that pop songs have limited durability. They can only surprise us so many times. Once we memorize all the moves—the fills, the solos, the vocal turns—we stop listening in the same way. The song no longer transports us. It's certainly possible to recapture that spark; classic rock is predicated on this capacity. But it's never the same as the first time—in love, in music, in anything. And so, over the years, Drooling Fanatics learn to conserve gratification. We're like those lab rats who parcel out our dope for maximum pleasure.

A Final Lullaby

So Josie and her little brother will learn to conserve gratification. They'll probably dream of being rock stars, too. Why not? They'll grow up with two parents who dreamed of being rock stars, in a house filled with instruments those parents can no longer play. And probably (this must be said) they won't be rock stars. How many of us get to be?

But what they will have, what we all get, is the chance to be Drooling Fanatics. And I hope they feel as I do—a bursting gratitude for those musicians brave enough to speak the first and final language of our hearts. Maybe Dayna Kurtz is right about that: the pleasures of listening to music may be greater, or purer anyway, than those of making it.

If they're lucky, someday they'll have children of their own. And they'll realize that you don't have to be a rock star to feel like a rock star. All you need is a soft little human with a sweet-smelling head who settles down at night with her bottle and says "Papa sing."

"What song do you want?" I say.

And Josie says "Corn," which means "Jimmy Crack Corn," or "Ring," which means "Hush, Little Baby," or, most often, "Coming," which means "She'll Be Coming 'Round the Mountain."

Then she says it again. "Papa sing."

And I get to say, "Sheesh, I thought you'd never ask."

Appendix A

The Official Drooling Fanatic Desert Island Playlist

(In no particular order—hey, this list took me fourteen months to settle on, and I'm still in anguish. . . .)

The Best of Gil Scott-Heron, Gil Scott-Heron

Salesmen and Racists, Ike Reilly

When We Were Big, Boris McCutcheon

Postcards from Downtown, Dayna Kurtz

My First Child, Nil Lara

Lonelyland, Bob Schneider

Fuse, Joe Henry

Let Freedom Ring, Chuck Prophet

Rabbit Songs, Hem

The Sons of Intemperance Offering, Phil Cody

Your Official Drooling Fanatic Desert Island Playlist

1. _____

2. _____

3. _____

4. _____

5. _____

6. _____

7. _____

8. _____

9. _____

10. _____

Appendix B
The Special Offer Hidden at the End of the Book!

In an effort to liquidate my CD collection all over you, I will send a free disc to any reader who sends me a SASE, along with certifiable evidence of his or her Drooling Fanaticism. This offer only good while supplies last! (So say the folks in Legal!) See www.stevenalmond.com for details! Really!

Acknowledgments

Giant Head-Banging Thank-Yous:

To all the musicians who appear in this book, particularly those who made the foolish but kind decision to allow me to invade their lives. Here's hoping everyone who arrives here will find your songs and consider themselves blessed. I certainly do.

To all those friends whose patient counsel helped rescue this silly book from the muck of my own poor judgments, and who inspired its composition: Billy Giraldi, Pat Flood, Keith Morris, Dave, Pete, and Mike Almond, Clay Martin, Holden Lewis, Tom DeMarchi, Eve Bridburg, Dave Blair, Michael Borum, Victor Cruz, Tim Huggins, Karl Iagnemma, Jenni Price, and Peter Keating.

To my wise and generous editor, Jill Schwartzman.

Last, and always, to my wife, Erin. If Kip Winger ever does get you back to his hotel room, babe, he'll be a fraction as lucky as I am.

Permission Acknowledgments

Grateful acknowledgment is made to the following for permission to reprint previously published material:

Alfred Music Publishing Co., Inc.: Excerpt from "Short Man's Room," words and music by Joe Henry, copyright © 1992 WB Music Corp., True North Music and Lemz Music. All rights administered by WB Music Corp. All rights reserved. Used by permission of Alfred Music Publishing Co., Inc.

Cherry Lane Music Company: Excerpt from "Africa," words and music by David Paich and Jeff Porcaro, copyright © 1982 Hudmar Publishing Co., Inc., and Rising Storm Music. All rights reserved. Used by permission.

Chrysalis Music Group USA: Excerpt from "Our Song" by Joe Henry, copyright © 2007 Chrysalis Music and Blood Count Music. All rights administered by Chrysalis Music. International copyright secured. All rights reserved. Used by permission of Chrysalis Music Group USA.

Hal Leonard Corporation: Excerpt from "Hello, Mary," words and music by David Baerwald, copyright © 1990 Almo Music Corp. and Zen of Iniquity. All rights controlled and administered by Almo Music Corp. All rights reserved. Used by permission of Hal Leonard Corporation.

Boris McCutcheon: Excerpts from "Hurt" and "Pony Ride," words and music by Boris McCutcheon, copyright © 2003, 2008 Cactusman Records (ASCAP). All rights reserved. Used by permission of Boris McCutcheon.

James McMurtry: Excerpt from "Rachel's Song," words and music by James McMurtry, copyright © 1995 Short Trip Music. All rights reserved. Used by permission.

Ike Reilly: Excerpts from "The War on the Terror and the Drugs," "I Don't Want What You Got (Goin' On)," "Commie Drives a Nova," and "What a Day," words and music by Ike Reilly, copyright © 2001, 2004, 2008 Siren Six Music. All rights reserved. Used by permission of Ike Reilly.

About the Author

STEVE ALMOND is the author of five previous books. He lives and rocks outside Boston with his wife and two children.

www.stevenalmond.com

About the Type

This book was set in Scala, a typeface designed by Martin
Majoor in 1991. It was originally designed for a music
company in the Netherlands and then was published
by the international type house FSI FontShop. Its
distinctive extended serifs add to the articulation of
the letterforms to make it a very readable typeface.